Teacher's Guide

Reading & Writing Excellence

KEYS TO STANDARDS-BASED ASSESSMENT

S0-AXJ-399

STECK-VAUGHN
BERRENT

A Harcourt Company

www.steck-vaughn.com

TABLE OF CONTENTS

Steck-Vaughn/Berrent is indebted to the following for permission to use material in this book:

page 17 "Little Girl, Be Careful What You Say" from THE COMPLETE POEMS OF CARL SANDBURG, copyright © 1970, 1969 by Lilian Steichen Sandburg, Trustee, reprinted by permission of Harcourt, Inc.

page 34 "Robots to the Rescue: How Newly Designed Robots May Soon Rock Your World" by Tina Adler/NGS Image Collection / from National Geographic World, No. 301, September 2000. Reprinted by permission of National Geographic Society.

page 46 "The Ocean Is Not a Dump" by Claudia Atticot. Used with permission from *TIME for Kids* magazine, © 2000, 2001.

page 50 "A Free Ride" – Reprinted by permission of CRICKET magazine, June 1999, Vol. 26, No. 9, © 1999 by Rebecca Aberg.

page 58 "A Touch of Genius" by Patricia Millman. Copyright © 2000 by Highlights for Children, Inc., Columbus, Ohio.

page 64 "Just a Sunday Drive in the Country" by Pete Hendley.

page 70 "Tracking the Wandering Albatross" by Jack Myers. Copyright © 2002 by Highlights for Children, Inc., Columbus, Ohio.

page 77 "Harriet Tubman" from *Honey, I Love*. Text copyright © 1978 by Eloise Greenfield. Used by permission of HarperCollins Publishers.

page 90 "Lost But Not Forgotten" by Stephen Wallenfels. Copyright © 2001 by Highlights for Children, Inc., Columbus, Ohio.

page 98 "Summers at Grandma's" – Reprinted by permission of CRICKET magazine, July 2000, Vol. 27, No. 11, © 2000 by Sharon Chmielarz.

page 104 "The Great Penguin Rescue" by Renee Skelton/NGS Image Collection / from National Geographic World, No. 305, January 2001. Reprinted by permission of National Geographic Society.

Photo Credits:
Cover photo: Larry Brownstein/©PhotoDisc; p.23 ©REUTERS/Dimitar Dilkoff/Hulton|Archive.; p.24 ©U.S. Treasury AP/Wide World Photo, Inc.; p.35 ©Atsushi Tsukada/AP/Wide World Photo, Inc.; p.47 ©The Press of Atlantic City/Dale Gerhard/AP/Wide World Photo, Inc.; p.58 ©Ron Thomas/AP/Wide World Photos, Inc.; p.70 ©Kevin Schafer/CORBIS; p.71 ©Osborne, B. OSF/Animals Animals; p.77 Courtesy the Library of Congress; p.104 ©Jon Hrusa/AP/Wide World Photo, Inc.; p.105 ©Mike Hutchings/REUTERS/Hulton|Archive; p.119 ©Larry Dale Gordon/Getty

Additional photography by: Steck-Vaughn Collection

STECK-VAUGHN BERRENT
A Harcourt Company

www.steck-vaughn.com

ISBN 0-7398-3963-2

Copyright © 2002 Steck-Vaughn Company

Published by Steck-Vaughn/Berrent Publications, a division of Steck-Vaughn Company.

1 2 3 4 5 6 7 8 9   TPO   06 05 04 03 02

About the Book

Reading & Writing Excellence is designed to prepare students for testing situations by providing integrated instruction for standards-based assessment. This book will refresh basic skills in reading and writing, with particular focus on writing in response to literature. The material in this book provides students with step-by-step instruction that will optimize success in classroom work as well as in testing situations.

A unique component of this book is the **Four *R*s** (**R**eady, **R**ead, **R**espond, **R**eview)—a strategy that will enable students to read selections, understand what they have read, and answer multiple-choice and open-ended questions about the reading material:

- *Ready*—Get ready to read by setting a purpose, previewing the selection, and making the predictions.
- *Read*—Read the selection as an active reader by anticipating outcomes, monitoring understanding, and confirming predictions.
- *Respond*—Read the question, think about it, and answer the question.
- *Review*—Check the answer.

The selections in this book include many genres typically encountered in standards-based reading tests, such as short stories, poetry, and non-fiction articles. The questions accompanying each passage represent the three levels of comprehension—literal, interpretive, and critical—and utilize the multiple-choice, short-answer, and essay formats. Furthermore, all the questions in the book are correlated to the NCTE Standards.

Special instruction is provided on using graphic organizers as prewriting aids for answering essay questions. Students are taught to conceptualize and categorize their ideas through the use of various graphic organizers, enabling them to write with more focus, organization, and clarity—an important and essential skill in all grades.

Speaking and listening are two other important areas covered in this book. A speaking prompt called "Speak Out" appears three times in the book to give students the opportunity to extend their knowledge of a selection in the form of a short speech. In addition, two passages in the book are used as *either* reading or listening selections. If you choose to conduct a listening activity, read the selection to the class instead of having them read it from the book. Then instruct the students to answer the questions without looking back at the selection.

Being well prepared for a test means having a definite strategy and knowing how to approach different types of questions. By using *Reading & Writing Excellence*, students will learn such strategies and achieve optimal performance in every reading and writing situation.

NCTE Standards

In order to aid teachers in determining strengths and weaknesses in their classrooms, the questions in *Reading & Writing Excellence* have been aligned to the standards developed by the National Council of Teachers of English (NCTE). Each standard is listed next to its corresponding answer in this Teacher's Guide. For easy reference, a chart of the standard correlations in the test section (Unit 4) can be found on page 128 of this guide.

You can find a description of the twelve NCTE Standards on this and the following page.

1. Students read a wide range of print and nonprint texts to build an understanding of texts, of themselves, and of the cultures of the United States and the world; to acquire new information; to respond to the needs and demands of society and the workplace; and for personal fulfillment. Among these texts are fiction and nonfiction, classic and contemporary works.

2. Students read a wide range of literature from many periods in many genres to build an understanding of the many dimensions (e.g., philosophical, ethical, aesthetic) of human experience.

3. Students apply a wide range of strategies to comprehend, interpret, evaluate, and appreciate texts. They draw on their prior experience, their interactions with other readers and writers, their knowledge of word meaning and of other texts, their word identification strategies, and their understanding of textual features (e.g., sound-letter correspondence, sentence structure, context, graphics).

4. Students adjust their use of spoken, written, and visual language (e.g., conventions, style, vocabulary) to communicate effectively with a variety of audiences and for different purposes.

5. Students employ a wide range of strategies as they write and use different writing process elements appropriately to communicate with different audiences for a variety of purposes.

6. Students apply knowledge of language structure, language conventions (e.g., spelling and punctuation), media techniques, figurative language, and genre to create, critique, and discuss print and nonprint texts.

7. Students conduct research on issues and interests by generating ideas and questions, and by posing problems. They gather, evaluate, and synthesize data from a variety of sources (e.g., print and nonprint texts, artifacts, people) to communicate their discoveries in ways that suit their purpose and audience.

8. Students use a variety of technological and information resources (e.g., libraries, databases, computer networks, video) to gather and synthesize information and to create and communicate knowledge.

9. Students develop an understanding of and respect for diversity in language use, patterns, and dialects across cultures, ethnic groups, geographic regions, and social roles.

10. Students whose first language is not English make use of their first language to develop competency in the English language arts and to develop understanding of content across the curriculum.

11. Students participate as knowledgeable, reflective, creative, and critical members of a variety of literacy communities.

12. Students use spoken, written, and visual language to accomplish their own purposes (e.g., for learning, enjoyment, persuasion, and the exchange of information).

4-Point Scoring Rubric for Essay Questions

A 4-point scoring rubric is provided below and on the following page. This rubric will prove helpful when grading your students' essay answers and determining writing abilities within the classroom.

4

The student:

► Responds effectively and accurately to all important parts of the question

► Shows a very good understanding of any related concepts involved with the question

► Maintains an efficient and consistent process and sticks to the topic

► Is well-organized and clearly shows understanding of the topic

► Offers insightful interpretations or extensions to ideas

► Shows a mature form of composition and communicates ideas very well

► Includes relevant details and examples from the text to further elaborate on points

3

The student:

► Responds effectively and accurately to most important parts of the question

► Shows a good understanding of major concepts but does not understand some ideas that are less important

► Maintains a consistent process and sticks to the topic for the most part

► Is organized and shows a good understanding of the topic

► Offers some interpretations or extensions to ideas

► Shows a form of composition and communicates ideas fairly well

► Includes some details and examples from the text to elaborate points

2

The student:

- ► Responds effectively and accurately to some important parts of the question
- ► Does not show a good understanding of the concepts
- ► Attempts to maintain a consistent process but drifts from the topic
- ► Attempts to be organized and shows some understanding of the topic
- ► Offers few interpretations or extensions to ideas
- ► Shows a form of composition with difficulty communicating ideas
- ► Includes very few details and examples from the text

1

The student:

- ► Shows very little understanding of the question and what is required
- ► Does not show an understanding of the concepts
- ► Does not maintain a consistent process and has difficulty sticking to the topic
- ► Is not organized and shows very little understanding of the topic
- ► Offers no interpretations or extensions to ideas
- ► Shows no form of composition and has a very hard time communicating ideas
- ► Includes no details or examples from the text

0

The student:

- ► Answers in an incorrect manner
- ► Writes an answer that is not decipherable or comprehensible
- ► Does not relate an answer that shows understanding of the topic or what is required
- ► Does not write an answer

UNIT 1

Introduction—Literal, Interpretive, and Critical Questions

Unit 1 focuses on answering questions at the three levels of comprehension—literal, interpretive, and critical. After a general introduction, the book takes students through a step-by-step process, explaining each level in detail. This ensures that they completely understand the differences among the three types of questions and have a strategy to successfully approach each. To ensure comprehension, you might wish to work with the students as they make their way through this unit rather than allowing them to do so independently.

Introduction to Literal Questions

The first part of the unit discusses how to answer a *literal question*, which involves the recall or recognition of information. Since the main problem in responding to a literal question is finding the answer in the selection, the instruction focuses on using key words in the question to help locate a specific piece of information. When no key words appear, students are told to look closely at the question and think carefully about what it is asking.

The instruction continues in the form of a reading passage followed by multiple-choice and short-answer questions. Accompanying each question is a detailed strategy for responding to it. This modeled instruction allows students to learn strategies for responding to this type of question in an actual reading situation.

Introduction to Interpretive Questions

The second part of the unit explains that students must determine meaning to answer an *interpretive question*. Now students must not only find information, but they must also use it to figure out the answers to questions. This task is compared to that of a detective, who must search for clues and then put the clues together to draw a conclusion. In this case, the student must examine the question, ascertain what information is necessary to answer it, search for the needed pieces of information, and then put this information together to form a response.

Once again the students receive modeled instruction in which multiple-choice and short-answer questions are asked about a passage.

Introduction to Critical Questions

The last section of the unit advises students to go beyond the text to respond to *critical questions*. For this type of question, they must think about what they have read and add what they know from their own experiences to evaluate, extend meaning, and make judgments about the material. The students are now instructed to put themselves in the role of a judge, who must form sound opinions and reach a decision about an issue. In this case, the students must study the information, decide on its importance, and make judgments about it.

The modeled instruction for this section includes two linked passages followed by short-answer questions only. In this case, each question requires that students write approximately one paragraph for their response. Students are also given the opportunity to "Speak Out" in this section and strengthen their communication skills by orally presenting a related topic to the class.

The following pages are picked up from Unit 1 in the Student Book for Level E. The correct answers to the multiple-choice questions have been filled in at the bottom of the page and possible answers to the short-answer questions have been added.

LEVEL 1: Find the Key
Introduction to Literal Questions

A literal question will ask you to recall or recognize information. The answer to the question is found in the selection.

Types of literal questions may include the following:

▶ Identifying details from the selection

▶ Identifying the order of events

▶ Identifying cause-and-effect situations

▶ Identifying character traits

Identify key words

The key to answering a literal question is to find out where the answer is. Think about where this information might appear in the selection. Then identify key words in the question that might also appear in the selection. For example, look at the following question:

What is the weather like in Brazil?

To answer this question, you would look for the key words *weather* and *Brazil* in the selection. If you cannot find these words, look for words that mean about the same thing. Instead of *weather*, you might look for *climate*. Or, you might look for words that tell about the weather, such as *hot* and *rainy*.

Find the clues

Sometimes you will not have key words to help you. Then you must think carefully about what the question is asking. Look at this question:

Which sentence tells the main idea of the passage?

Here there are no key words to look for, but the answer can still be found in the selection. First, you must know what a *main idea* is. It is the most important idea in the selection. So you would look for the one sentence that clearly tells what the whole selection is about.

Answering Literal Questions

Now you will learn how to answer literal questions about a story. Be sure to follow the **Four *R*s:**

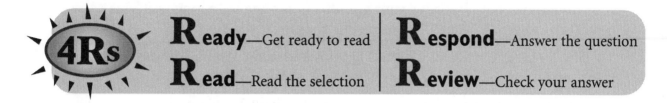

4Rs

Ready—Get ready to read   **R**espond—Answer the question

Read—Read the selection   **R**eview—Check your answer

DIRECTIONS: Read this story about a boy who comes across an old photograph. Then answer questions 1 through 8.

A Lesson Through Pictures

by Susan Luton

The second week of summer vacation started with a downpour early in the morning. But by the time Randy was out of bed and dressed, the sky had turned blue. "Yes!" he said as he looked out the window. He and J.D., his best friend, had plans to meet at the park to shoot baskets.

Randy's mom was in the kitchen when he went downstairs. "After you eat, you need to help me take some boxes to the attic," she said.

"But I'm supposed to meet J.D. at the park."

"You'll be finished in time," she said with a smile. Randy was glad his mother was home for the summer. She could drive him and his friends places. But it also meant that she often had chores for him to do.

"Be sure to rinse your dishes," she called on her way down the hall. She was headed for a room his father used for an office. Randy quickly finished his breakfast, rinsed the dishes, and joined his mother.

The room was a mess. There were so many half-filled boxes everywhere that it was hard to find a place to step. "Why are we moving all this stuff?" Randy asked.

"You know that tomorrow your grandpa is coming for a long visit," his mother answered. "Well, I'm getting this room ready for him."

She pointed to a box of old photographs and said, "Would you start by taking that one to my bedroom? I'll have Dad look through it later."

On his way up the stairs, Randy happened to look at the photographs at the top of the box. There were many old black-and-white photographs. Some of the photos were of angry-looking people. A young man who looked like his cousin was in most of these. In one photo, he and a group of other young black and white men and women were being yelled at by an angry mob. The young man's group had signs with city names he didn't recognize and the phrase "Civil Rights" in large letters.

Randy's mother came up the stairs with another box.

"Mom, who's the guy in all the pictures?"

"That's your uncle John."

Randy held the picture with his uncle being yelled at and stared at it. His uncle looked angry and sad and proud all at the same time.

"Why is everyone so angry?"

"Your uncle was at a civil rights protest. People were angry because not everyone believed in the things your uncle believed. Those angry people did not believe that African-Americans should be treated the same way white people were treated. Talk to your dad about this when he gets home."

Randy and J.D. got to the park at the same time. They shot baskets until they were hot and sweaty. Then they stretched out in the shade of a gigantic oak tree. The ground still felt a little wet from the big rain.

Randy broke the silence. "J.D., what do you know about civil rights protests back when our parents were young?"

"I know my parents were in a few. My aunts and uncles too. They were tired of being mistreated and getting second-hand things. Even in their schools, they got old books that the white schools didn't want anymore."

All the way home Randy thought about what J.D. said.

Randy's dad was sitting on the patio with his mom. Randy tossed him the basketball and asked, "Dad, why do you have all those old pictures of Uncle John in the box?"

"Your grandfather gave them to me when John graduated from college and moved out on his own. He told me to always remember how important it is to fight for what you believe in. John saw that he was given advantages that African-American boys were not given. He knew his life was a lot easier because of this. John just didn't think it was fair the way many people treated African-Americans. A lot of people didn't agree with John, and he took some risks to fight for his beliefs. In the end, most people have come to agree with John's way of thinking."

"But Uncle John could have been hurt. Those people look really angry!"

"Yes, he could have been hurt. But he felt that thousands of Americans had already been hurt worse than anything that would happen to him by protesting."

That night Randy's dad came into his bedroom.

"I want you to have this," he said to Randy. It was the photograph of John in which he looked angry and sad and proud all at once. "Maybe one day you'll stand up for something you believe in, like your uncle did. If you do, I want you to look at this picture and know that people *can* make a difference."

Randy said, "I'm not sure I ever want to be in front of people who are so angry at me. But I'm glad that J.D. and I get to go to the same school and can be friends."

"Me too," his dad said as he left the room.

DIRECTIONS: Read each question carefully. Darken the circle at the bottom of the page or write your answer on the lines.

I Over what period of time does this story take place?

A One morning

B One day

C One week

D One summer

Find the Key

This question asks about the setting of the story. The setting of a story is where and *when* it takes place. Read the question and the choices carefully. Then go back and scan the story. Keep track of how much time passes. Look at the beginning, middle, and end. When does the story begin? What time of day is it? When does the story end? What time of day is it?

2 Which of the following *best* describes Randy?

F He likes to ask questions.

G He likes to sleep late.

H He likes to help around the house.

J He likes his grandpa to visit.

Find the Key

This question asks you to identify character traits. First, read the choices carefully. Some of the choices might describe Randy, but you have to determine which of them is the *best.* As you skim the story, do two things: Keep the choices in mind and pay attention to Randy's actions. His actions will give you the answer to this question.

Answers

1 Ⓐ ● Ⓒ Ⓓ	2 ● Ⓖ Ⓗ Ⓙ
Standards 1,3	**Standards 1,3**

3 Which event happened *first* in the story?

A Randy shot baskets with J.D.

B Randy asked J.D. about civil rights.

C Randy's dad gave him a photograph of his uncle.

D Randy looked at old photographs.

Find the Key

This question asks you to put events in the order that they happened. You probably have a good idea just from reading the story. Go back and find each event in the story. Then put the events in order. Which event was the *first* to happen?

4 At the end of the story, Randy is thankful that—

F his grandpa gave the photographs to his father

G he and J.D. live close to each other

H his mom gets to stay home during the summer

J he and J.D. go to the same school

Find the Key

Now you must identify details. Start by eliminating any answers you know are wrong because they are not mentioned in the story. Then, to find the right answer, reread the end of the story. Think about what Randy says at the end and put it together with the story's theme, or the message the author is giving the reader.

Answers

3 Ⓐ Ⓑ Ⓒ ●	4 Ⓕ Ⓖ Ⓗ ●
Standards 1,3	**Standards 1,3**

5 Why was Randy happy that the weather had changed?

Randy was happy that the rain had stopped because he knew he would get to play

basketball with J.D.

Standards 1,3,4,5,6

Find the Key

This is a cause-and-effect question. Now, instead of choosing an answer, you will write your own answer to the question. Read the question carefully. Then reread the first part of the story where it says the sky turned blue. What was Randy going to get to do since the weather had changed? Write your answer in a complete sentence.

6 What is the setting of the beginning of the story?

The beginning of the story takes place in Randy's house in the morning during

the second week of summer vacation.

Standards 1,3,4,5,6

Find the Key

Remember, the setting of a story is where and when it takes place. Here, you are asked to tell the setting of the beginning of the story. Where and when does the first half of the story take place? The answer is right in the story. Read the first few paragraphs again. Be sure to write your answer in a complete sentence.

7 How did Randy's Uncle John feel about the way African-Americans were treated?

Randy's Uncle John felt that African-Americans were treated unfairly. He wanted

things to change.

Standards 1,3,4,5,6

Find the Key

This question asks you to identify details from the story. The answer is in the story. Read the part of the story where Randy's father talks about John. He explains why John took part in civil rights protests. Look for words that describe how John *feels* about certain things.

8 Why does Randy's father give him the photograph at the end of the story?

He gave Randy the photograph so that Randy will be reminded that people can

make a difference when they stand up for their beliefs.

Standards 1,3,4,5,6

Find the Key

This is another cause-and-effect question. Look back at the story and read the last few paragraphs. You will find the answer here. Read what Randy's father says to Randy. What is the main point he makes to his son when he gives Randy the photograph?

LEVEL 2: Turn the Lock
Introduction to
Interpretive Questions

A detective looks at different pieces of information to find answers. When you answer an interpretive question, you put together different pieces of a selection to determine its meaning.

Types of interpretive questions may include the following:

► Interpreting character traits

► Interpreting vocabulary

► Determining the main idea

► Summarizing information

► Drawing conclusions

Unlock the answer

To answer an interpretive question, you must become a detective. Before a detective can look for clues, he or she must know what to look for. You can tell what to look for by examining the question.

Suppose you had to answer a question about *Beauty and the Beast,* a story in which a beautiful young woman falls in love with a beast. Look at the following question:

Why does the young woman fall in love with the beast?

The answer will not be right there in the story for you to find. You have to think carefully about what you have read to figure it out. You would need to reread the parts where the young woman and the beast talk to each other. How does the beast act toward the young woman throughout the story?

Put the clues together

After you have reread parts of the selection, think about what you have read. Then, like the detective, put the clues together to draw a conclusion.

In the question above, you might find that the beast was kind and gentle with the young woman. Perhaps they shared things in common. These clues show you that the woman could overlook the beast's appearance and fall in love with his inner self.

Answering Interpretive Questions

Now you will learn how to answer interpretive questions about a poem.
Remember to follow the **Four *R*s:**

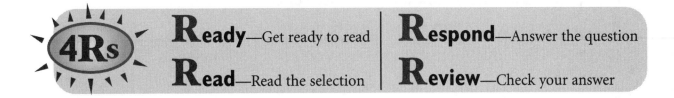

4Rs   **R**eady—Get ready to read   **R**espond—Answer the question
          Read—Read the selection   **R**eview—Check your answer

DIRECTIONS: Read this poem about advice that is given to a girl. Then answer questions 1 through 8.

Little Girl, Be Careful What You Say

by Carl Sandburg

Little girl, be careful what you say
when you make talk with words, words—
for words are made of syllables
and syllables, child, are made of air—
and air is so thin—air is the breath of God—
air is *finer* than fire or mist,
finer than water or moonlight,
finer than spider-webs in the moon,
finer than water-flowers in the morning:
    and words are strong, too,
    stronger than rocks or steel
stronger than potatoes, corn, fish, cattle,
and soft, too, soft as little pigeon-eggs,
soft as the music of hummingbird wings.
    So, little girl, when you speak greetings,
when you tell jokes, make wishes or prayers,
    be careful, be careless, be careful,
    be what you wish to be.

DIRECTIONS: Read each question carefully. Darken the circle at the bottom of the page or write your answer on the lines.

1 Which is the *best* summary of the poem?

   A A poet tells a little girl how words are made of air.

   B A poet explains to a little girl why words are strong.

   C A poet tells a little girl that she will use words to greet people and tell jokes.

   D A poet compares words to other things so that a little girl can understand how important they are.

Turn the Lock

This question asks you to summarize the poem. A summary tells only the main points and most important details of a selection. It is much shorter than a retelling. It is never made up of only one or a few details. What is most important about what the poet is telling the little girl? Which of the answer options can be eliminated because they are made up of only one or a few details?

2 In the poem, the word *finer* means—

   F larger

   G more delicate

   H better quality

   J stronger

Turn the Lock

This is a vocabulary question. You have probably heard the word *finer* many times. This word has several meanings. You must decide which meaning is being used in the poem. Think about the things that the poet is comparing to air as he uses the word *fine*. What quality or qualities do these things have in common?

Answers

1 Ⓐ Ⓑ Ⓒ ●	2 Ⓕ ● Ⓗ Ⓙ
Standards 1,3	Standards 1,3,6

3 Which word *best* describes the tone of the poem?

   A sad

   B mysterious

   C serious

   D humorous

Turn the Lock

The tone of a selection is the mood that the author creates. The tone will never be stated in the selection. You must figure it out from the writer's choice of words and how they are put together. To find the tone of this poem, read it silently or in a quiet voice as if you were the poet actually talking to the little girl.

4 What is another good title for this poem?

   F "The Power of Words"

   G "Words Are Made of Air"

   H "How to Talk Well"

   J "What Is Fine, Strong, and Soft?"

Turn the Lock

The title of a poem usually tells the main idea of the poem. The main idea is what the poem is mostly about. Read each choice to see which title best tells the poem's main idea. Make sure that the title you choose is not about just part of the poem, but that it is about the whole poem.

Answers

3 Ⓐ Ⓑ ● Ⓓ	4 ● Ⓖ Ⓗ Ⓙ
Standards 1,3	**Standards 1,3**

5 What do you think is the relationship of the poet to the little girl? Explain your answer.

<u>Students may state that the poet knows the girl because he speaks with</u>

<u>tenderness and is trying to teach her a lesson. They may also state that the poet</u>

<u>does not know the girl because he uses the formal title "little girl" with her.</u>

Standards 1,3,4,5,6

Turn the Lock

This question asks you to draw a conclusion about the poem. No word in the poem tells the reader what the relationship is between the poet and the little girl. You must look for clues in the poem's words and tone. Does the poet talk to her as if they are strangers or as if they know each other? Does he talk to her formally or informally? Are his words harsh, or are they tender?

6 The poet says that words are stronger than potatoes, corn, fish, and cattle. Why does he consider these things strong?

<u>Answers should include that these things are strong in a way that you would</u>

<u>not normally think of—strong because they are foods that people need to stay</u>

<u>alive.</u>

Standards 1,3,4,5,6

Turn the Lock

Here you must compare and contrast a little bit. Think about the four things mentioned. Remember that writers often use language, including comparisons, to make readers consider something in a new or unexpected way. What do these four things have in common? How would they be considered *strong*?

7 How important are words to the poet? Explain.

Words are very important to the poet. He describes words as being fine, strong,

and soft. All of these qualities make you pay attention to things.

Standards 1,3,4,5,6

Turn the Lock

Again, you must draw a conclusion from the information in the poem. What comparisons does the poet make? What descriptions does he use? Skim the poem to look for words that might be useful clues in answering this question. Your answer should be at least one complete sentence that includes your description of the poet's feelings about words, as well as the clues you found that made you come to that conclusion.

8 Why does the poet compare words to delicate things, like pigeon-eggs and hummingbird wings?

Answers should include that the poet tells the girl to be careful of what she says.

Words are delicate. You must also be careful with delicate things, like pigeon-eggs

and hummingbird wings.

Standards 1,3,4,5,6

Turn the Lock

This is a main idea question. You will not find the answer directly stated in the poem. Think about the question. What advice is the poet giving the girl? Read the beginning and ending of the poem. How does this relate to delicate things?

LEVEL 3: Open the Door
Introduction to Critical Questions

For a critical question, you must go beyond the words on the page. You bring in your own experiences to evaluate and extend meaning. You also make judgments about what you have read.

Types of critical questions may include the following:

▶ Analyzing the situation

▶ Predicting outcomes

▶ Determining the author's purpose

▶ Extending the passage

▶ Evaluating the passage

Step through the door

Now, you are going to become a judge. You will still look for clues to answer a question. But you will also study the information, decide how important it is, and make judgments about it.

Let's go back to the story *Beauty and the Beast.* Look at this question:

**Do you think that a woman could actually fall in love
with an ugly-looking beast? Why or why not?**

There is no way to find the answer in the story. Even putting together clues will not give you the answer. This question is asking for your opinion. You must make a judgment based on the story and on your own experiences.

Make a case

A judge never makes a hasty decision, and neither should you. Think about the people you love. Why do you love them? Are your feelings based on what they look like?

Next, think about the story. Even though it is a fairy tale, are the characters believable? Do you think that the young woman could fall in love with the beast?

Form your opinion and make a judgment in order to answer the question.

Answering Critical Questions

Now you will learn how to answer critical questions about two selections. Don't forget to follow the **Four *R*s:**

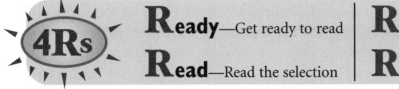

4Rs

Ready—Get ready to read

Respond—Answer the question

Read—Read the selection

Review—Check your answer

DIRECTIONS: Read this article about coins and coin collecting. Then read the ad that follows it. Then answer questions I and 2.

A Bridge Across Time

Have you ever held something that was very old? It might have been a photograph of a great-great-grandfather or a ring worn by a great-aunt. Or you might have held your mother's first drawing or a lock of hair from your father's first haircut.

Some of us have been lucky enough to hold an object that has survived over many years. This makes the past seem a little closer to the present. Objects can be bridges across time. This is one reason why many people have an interest in numismatics—the study and collecting of coins, paper money, medals, and tokens. Of these four items, coins are probably studied and collected most often.

A few people are professional coin collectors, but most collect coins as a hobby. Collectors may enjoy coins because of how rare they are. They also may take pleasure in the images on the coins. Some of the images are beautiful, just as works of art are. All images on coins reflect history in one way or another.

A coin is considered rare when fewer copies of it exist than are wanted by collectors. Usually, the rarer a coin is, the greater its value is. The value of a coin is the price a coin dealer would charge for it. The price depends on how many coins exist and how many people want them.

Images have been found on coins for more than 2,000 years. Gods and goddesses were portrayed on most coins of ancient Greece. Coins of the Roman Empire were often stamped with images of emperors. In the United States, monuments, bald eagles, and buffaloes have appeared on coins. You will also find many different U.S. leaders.

The images on coins provide clues about the history of the empire or nation that produced the coins. Consider the images on a series of U.S. quarters that started being produced in 1999. The quarters are part of the 50 States Commemorative Coin Program Act. Commemorative means "serving to honor a person, place, or event." And that is exactly what these quarters do. In 2008, the year the U.S. Mint will complete the series, there will be one quarter honoring each state. George Washington will still appear on the face of each quarter, but the eagle that has been on the back of quarters for many years will be gone. In its place you will see a design that was developed by the state being honored.

The Delaware quarter was the first in the series to be prduced. The back of this quarter potrays the historic horseback ride of Caesar Rodney. Rodney was an important figure in early U.S. history. Although he was very ill, he rode a horse 80 miles through bad weather on a serious mission to Philadelphia. That mission was to cast the deciding vote in favor of the nation's independence.

The production of quarters for the other states follows the order in which the states joined the Union. Alaska and Hawaii quarters will be made last.

Think of all the historical clues that will be on these special U.S. quarters. Then imagine this: A 10-year-old girl living 200 years from now is holding one of these quarters before placing it in her coin collection. After studying the coin's images, she decides to learn more about U.S. history. The coin and her interest in numismatics will connect her to the past, which is your present.

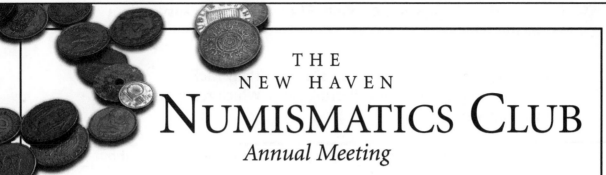

THE NEW HAVEN
NUMISMATICS CLUB
Annual Meeting

The New Haven Numismatics Club will hold its annual meeting in the Conference Room of the Royal Oaks Hotel. The meeting is open to the public.

Topic:	**Coin Collecting for Young People**
Date:	**October 20**
Time:	**6:30 P.M.–8:00 P.M.**
Address:	**1400 South Second Street**

The New Haven Numismatics Club is celebrating its twentieth anniversary at this meeting. In our effort to encourage young people to become numismatists (coin collectors), we have invited Brittany McKenzie to give a talk.

Brittany began collecting coins when she was seven years old. Now nineteen, she has a huge collection of old coins. She has written several articles about coins with historical value. She also has a web site that is full of information about how to find old coins.

With her talk and coin collection exhibit, Brittany hopes to get young people interested in becoming coin collectors. She will describe the benefits of collecting coins, including:

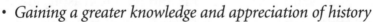
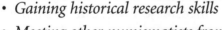
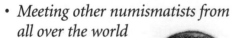

- *Gaining a greater knowledge and appreciation of history*
- *Gaining historical research skills*
- *Meeting other numismatists from all over the world*

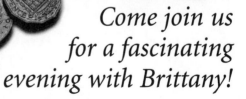

Come join us for a fascinating evening with Brittany!

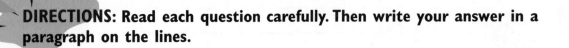

DIRECTIONS: Read each question carefully. Then write your answer in a paragraph on the lines.

1 Both the author of "A Bridge Across Time" and Brittany McKenzie seem to favor one reason in particular for collecting coins. Which reason is this? Support your answer.

Students should mention that most people collect coins to learn about the past.

Students should use details from the article and the ad to back up their

assertions.

Standards 1,3,4,5,6,7,11

_____

_____

_____

_____

Open the Door

Here you must make a connection between the two passages you just read. First, skim both selections and list the reasons given for collecting coins. Then, check your lists to see if some ideas are mentioned repeatedly. Decide which reason for coin collecting seems to be favored by the author of "A Bridge Across Time" and Brittany McKenzie. Determine which parts of the selections support your answer.

2 Which details in "A Bridge Across Time" do you think would help Brittany McKenzie prepare her speech for The New Haven Numismatics Club's annual meeting?

Answers should include how history can come alive for young people when objects

are involved in the learning and teaching of history. The first and last paragraphs

of "Numismatics" can be used as well.

Standards 1,3,4,5,6,7,11

_____

_____

_____

_____

Open the Door

This question again asks you to make a connection between the two passages. You must find information in the first passage that is relevant to the second passage. Read the ad again. Pay particular attention to what Brittany would like to accomplish at the meeting. Next, reread "A Bridge Across Time." Which information in the selection would be most appealing to young people?

Speak Out

You have read about coin collecting and why people do it as a hobby. What is a hobby you enjoy or what is a hobby you would like to try? Prepare a short speech about this hobby and the benefits of it. Then give your speech to the class.

Summary

In this unit, you have learned how to answer questions at three "key" levels of comprehension.

Find the Key

"Literal"

Look for information

Turn the Lock

"Interpretive"

Determine meaning

Open the Door

"Critical"

Go beyond the text

Remember that no matter what type of question you answer, you should always use the **Four *R*s:** Ready, Read, Respond, Review.

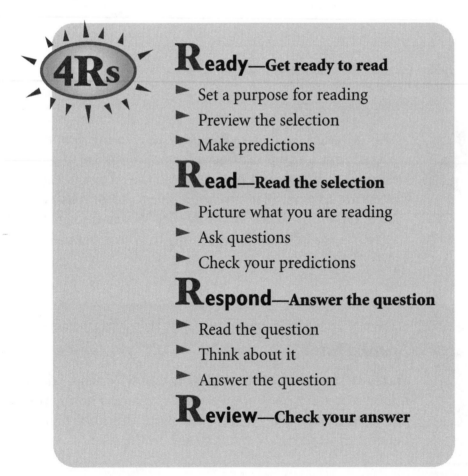

4Rs

Ready—**Get ready to read**
- Set a purpose for reading
- Preview the selection
- Make predictions

Read—**Read the selection**
- Picture what you are reading
- Ask questions
- Check your predictions

Respond—**Answer the question**
- Read the question
- Think about it
- Answer the question

Review—**Check your answer**

UNIT 2
Introduction— Graphic Organizers

Unit 2 presents instruction on graphic organizers as prewriting aids for responding to essay questions. Graphic organizers provide conceptual frames for students to collect ideas and categorize them. Within those frames, students can see relationships and make connections. Graphic organizers are powerful thinking tools. They can help students organize both information they gather during reading as well as thoughts they might generate for writing and speaking.

As with Unit 1, it might be helpful to work with the students as they make their way through this unit rather than allowing them to do so independently. As you do this, model each graphic organizer on the blackboard with the class before asking them to fill in the organizer themselves. Make sure that students are comfortable with each organizer so that they will be able to use it independently with other selections.

There are six graphic organizers presented in this unit. For each, the students first read a passage, then receive instruction on the particular graphic organizer, and finally learn how to fill in the organizer as a prewriting activity to help answer an essay question about the passage. The graphic organizers presented are as follows:

▶ *Character Traits Web*—Students learn that a web can help them connect ideas. The Character Traits Web is an aid to help them organize their thoughts about a particular character by listing character traits and then giving an event in the story that illustrates that trait.

▶ *Main Idea Map*—The instruction defines main idea as the most important idea in a passage. Students learn that the Main Idea Map is an organizer in which they record the main idea, its subtopics, and the details for each subtopic.

▶ *Story Map*—Students learn about the different parts of a story: setting, character, problem, events, and solution. They then fill in a Story Map by listing the different parts of a particular story.

▶ *Sequence Map*—Students discover how a Sequence Map can help them organize events by placing them in the order in which they occurred and listing details about each event.

▶ *Cause and Effect Map*—The instruction defines a *cause* as why something happened and an *effect* as what happened as a result. Students learn how to list single causes and their effects.

▶ *Venn Diagram*—Students learn how a Venn Diagram can help them answer an essay question requiring a comparison.

Initially, students will need a great deal of guidance in filling in the graphic organizers. The more they practice and become familiar with the organizers, the less dependent they will ultimately be on you in completing them.

Encourage students to use these graphic organizers with other selections. Point out that a Story Map can only be used with fiction selections and a Main Idea Map is usually used with nonfiction writing. However, all graphic organizers are versatile. You might, for example, mention that while a Character Traits Web is often used with fiction selections, it might also be helpful with biographies. A Sequence Map can be used with any selection that has events occurring in a certain order. In addition, a Cause and Effect Map and a Venn Diagram are helpful with both fiction and nonfiction selections.

As students continue to use these graphic organizers, they will learn to recognize patterns in a variety of texts as well as recurring relationships and connections. Be sure to point out to students that the graphic organizers are only samples and examples. Students should feel free to make up their own charts, diagrams, and webs based on what works for them.

Once students have written their essays based on the information they wrote in the graphic organizer, they can check their work on page 56 of the Student Book. There is an editing and revising checklist on this page to help them evaluate their essays and make improvements as necessary. You might want to review this checklist with your class when you begin teaching this unit.

In addition, another "Speak Out" can be found in Unit 2, at the end of the lesson on the Main Idea Map.

The following pages are picked up from Unit 2 in the Student Book for Level E. Possible completions of the graphic organizers have been added, as well as requirements for the essay answers. Remember to use the 4-point rubric on pages 6 and 7 of this Teacher's Guide to help you monitor your students' writing abilities and individual strengths and weaknesses.

2 Graphic Organizers: The Key to Answering Essay Questions

The Essay Question

In Unit 1 you answered both multiple-choice and short-answer questions. Another type of test question is an essay question. For an essay question, you must write a few paragraphs. Essay questions often require more thought than other types of questions. You must recall and understand details of the passage you just read.

Get Organized!

You know how hard it is to find something in a messy drawer. You look and look, but the thing you are looking for escapes you in the clutter. However, finding something in a well-organized drawer is very easy. In the same way, you can answer an essay question more easily if you are organized before you begin to write.

A **graphic organizer** is a picture that lets you put your ideas in order. A graphic organizer helps you gather the information you need to answer your essay question. Once you organize your thoughts and ideas, it will be easier for you to write your essay.

In this unit, you will learn how to use different kinds of graphic organizers to answer essay questions. But first, here are some things to think about before you begin to write.

Before You Write

Before you write anything, ask yourself some questions:

1. *What is my topic?* What will you be writing about? State the topic in a few words. This will help you focus your writing.

2. *Why am I writing?* Think about the purpose of the essay. Usually you write to explain, persuade, entertain, or describe something.

3. *Who will read my writing?* This is your audience. Your teacher will probably be your audience for a test.

This page may not be reproduced without permission of Steck-Vaughn/Berrent.

DIRECTIONS: Read the following story about a boy named Robbie and his grandmother. Then you will use a Character Traits Web. It will help you describe Robbie.

Cooking for Abuelita

"Roberto Vega, you're going to break me someday."

Robbie glanced at his grandmother's face. It gave him clues to how serious her words were. If she was smiling her strange smile that turned down instead of up, then he didn't worry. But if her features were pulled together tightly, then he knew he'd better pay attention to what she said next. "Uh-oh," he thought when he saw the deep lines on her frowning face.

All he'd done was ask for ten dollars to go to the movies with his friends. You'd have thought he was asking for ten *hundred* dollars.

"Roberto, you can't keep spending money like this," his grandmother said. "I'm sorry, but I just don't have it."

"But Abuelita, I don't ask you for much money. It's just that I spent the last of my lawn mowing money last week. And I really want to see the movie."

"Well, Roberto, I can't spare the ten dollars right now. You're going to have to find a cold-weather way to make some spending money."

Robbie's grandmother turned and walked slowly toward her room. He could tell from her sighs that the arthritis in her knees was bothering her. He went to his room and threw himself on his bed. His eyes were just an inch from his favorite square of the patchwork quilt his grandmother had made him. The square was from a flowered blouse his mom used to wear—before she got so sick that she wore only gowns and robes.

"Not fair. Not fair. Not fair." Robbie said the words quietly, over and over. Sometimes it was hard to look at that flowered square on the quilt because it made him miss his mom even more. At the same time, looking at it helped keep the memory of her from getting cloudy.

Robbie sat up and took out a notebook and pen from the nightstand drawer. He wrote how he felt in the notebook.

It's not fair that Mom and Dad divorced when I was a baby and Dad went back to San Juan. It's not fair that Mom is gone. But it's fair that Abuelita wanted me to live with her. It's fair that she cooks like Mom and takes care of me. But it's not fair that she refuses to call me Robbie like Mom did. It's not fair that her knees hurt her. AND IT'S NOT FAIR THAT SHE DOES NOT HAVE MONEY TO GIVE ME TO GO TO THE MOVIES.

Robbie put down the notebook and looked at the posters on the ceiling. They were travel posters of Puerto Rico. He'd used them for an oral report in class then decided to hang them in his room. He looked carefully at the man on a sailboat in one of the posters and wondered if his father ever felt like he did right now.

"How can I feel sad and mad and disappointed—and sorry for Abuelita—all at the same time?" he thought.

Robbie went to his grandmother's door. "Abuelita?" he said softly.

"Yes, Roberto?" She was sitting in a chair with her feet on a stool.

"How about if I'm the main cook tonight? You can tell me what to do from a kitchen chair."

"Thank you, Roberto," she said. "I was just sitting here thinking about your mother and how unfair life can be. It takes a lot of courage on our part to carry on, don't you think?"

"I guess so. But when you're naming everything that's unfair, it helps when you mix in the fair things," Robbie said, and Abuelita smiled.

Character Traits Web

A **Character Traits Web** helps you organize your thoughts about what a character is like. In this organizer, the name of the character goes in the box at the top. A trait, or word that describes the character, goes on each of four lines underneath. Then, in each of four boxes at the bottom, write an event from the story that shows that character's trait.

Read the essay question and instructions on page 33.

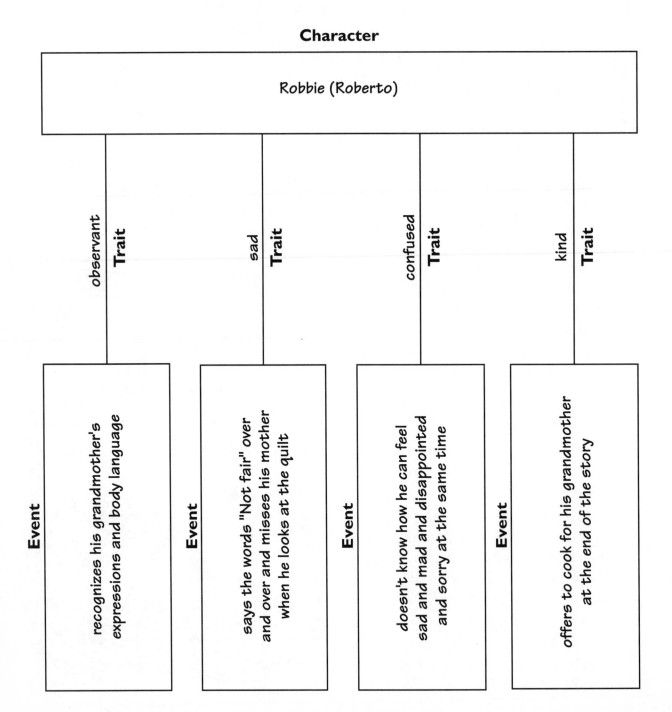

Character

Robbie (Roberto)

Trait
observant

Trait
sad

Trait
confused

Trait
kind

Event
recognizes his grandmother's expressions and body language

Event
says the words "Not fair" over and over and misses his mother when he looks at the quilt

Event
doesn't know how he can feel sad and mad and disappointed and sorry at the same time

Event
offers to cook for his grandmother at the end of the story

Essay Question: Discuss at least four different character traits that describe Robbie. Use events from the story to explain each of these traits. Then, tell which trait you think *best* describes Robbie.

1. You must describe Robbie. Since Robbie is the character you will be writing about, write his name in the box at the top of the organizer.

2. Next, think about words you could use to describe Robbie. To help you, look back at the things that Robbie says, thinks, and does. Write a character trait on each of the lines underneath the box at the top.

3. Now, in each of the boxes at the bottom, write an event from the story that shows the character trait. Find these events by skimming through the story again.

Now that you have filled in the **Character Traits Web,** use it to answer the essay question at the top of the page. Write your answer on a separate sheet of paper.

> **ANSWER** Answers will vary. Students should choose four appropriate words to describe Robbie and use an event from the story to show how he exhibited each character trait. For example, students might say that Robbie is confused. As the event, they could mention how Robbie asked himself how he could feel sad, mad, disappointed, and sorry for his grandmother at the same time. They must tell which trait they think *best describes* Robbie and why. Standards 1,3,4,5,6,7,11

Open the Door

This question asks you to analyze a character, or tell what you think of him, by describing character traits. This is a critical question. You must go beyond the text and make a judgment about what you have read. You must also choose which trait best describes Robbie.

Look at the graphic organizer you just filled in. Use the traits you named in the organizer. Write about each trait and include an event from the story that shows this trait. Then write a few sentences about which trait describes Robbie the best, and why.

DIRECTIONS: Read the following article about robots. Then you will use a Main Idea Map. It will help you explain why scientists create robots.

Robots to the Rescue:

How Newly Designed Robots May Soon Rock Your World

by Tina Adler

It's the weekend, and you're playing catch with Aibo, your robotic dog. Your sister is reading on the porch while the robotic lawn mower cuts the grass. A few minutes later, another robot rolls out the front door, telling the two of you it's time for lunch.

Not your typical Saturday? Not yet. But all these robots are real—and if scientists have their way, they'll one day be as common as televisions.

In the 1920s a science fiction writer "invented" the word *robot*. The first robots were evil characters in a play. By the 1960s, companies had developed real but very simple robots to work in factories, relieving humans from many tedious or dangerous jobs. Robot technology has come a long way since then.

Today's robots are tough, cute, complex, responsive, and even "emotional." Some resemble humans; others look like insects. But no matter what cool things robots can do, all have one common purpose: making humans' lives better.

A robot is a mechanical device that performs actions, often in response to its surroundings. Usually operated by computer, a robot has software that tells it how to respond to what its sensors and cameras feel or see.

Robots can also be programmed to "grow up," or change over time. They have internal clocks that track how long they have been in use. One doll now being sold babbles like a 6-month-old when it's new, but eventually it talks like a 2-year-old. (But don't expect potty training!)

Robots definitely make cool toys, but that's not why scientists are creating most of them. Scientists have to build complex robots step-by-step. They develop one technology, such as recognizing emotions, then another, such as learning. Put those two together, and you could have a robotic nurse in a hospital that recognizes when a patient is in pain and knows how to find the doctor. (For instance, after working in the hospital for two months, the robot would learn that every Tuesday afternoon the doctor could be found in her office doing paperwork.)

With all the awesome things that robots can do, why aren't they more common? "One big problem is that many need their batteries recharged after just a few hours," explains Mark Tilden of Los Alamos National Laboratory in Santa Fe, New Mexico. "And they're still not foolproof to operate."

Scientists still need to work out a few glitches. "But robots will eventually become as common as refrigerators," predicts Rodney Brooks, a scientist at the Massachusetts Institute of Technology in Boston. You won't call them robots, though, any more than you'd call a microwave oven a computer, though it has a computer in it. One thing's for sure: You *will* call them cool—especially when you program them to clean your room, help do your homework, or make you a pizza!

Main Idea Map

A **Main Idea Map** helps you organize a selection's main idea, or what the selection is about. In this organizer, the main idea goes in the box at the top. Under the box is a circle for each subtopic, or supporting idea. You can add as many circles as you need. Then, under each subtopic is a box for details about the subtopic.

Read the essay question and instructions on page 37.

Main Idea

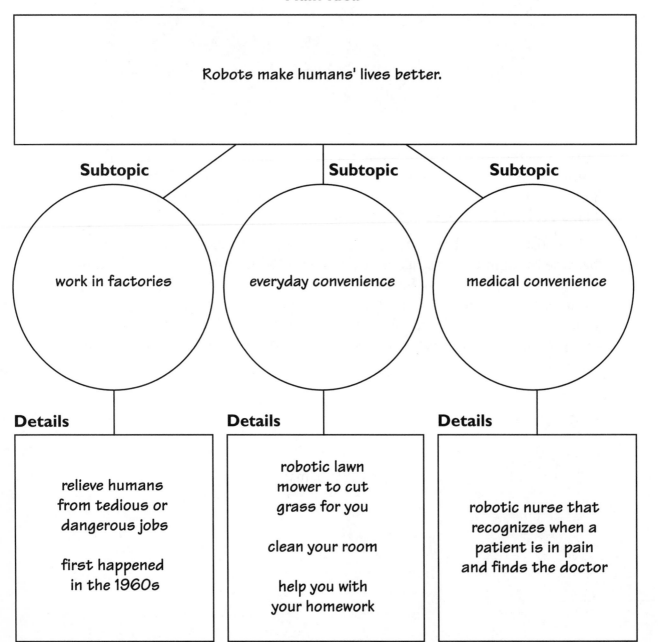

Robots make humans' lives better.

Subtopic

work in factories

Subtopic

everyday convenience

Subtopic

medical convenience

Details

relieve humans from tedious or dangerous jobs

first happened in the 1960s

Details

robotic lawn mower to cut grass for you

clean your room

help you with your homework

Details

robotic nurse that recognizes when a patient is in pain and finds the doctor

Essay Question: What is the main reason scientists create robots? Use details and examples from the article to support your answer.

1. The answer to the question can be found in the fourth paragraph of the article. Write this as the main idea in the box at the top.

2. Next, you have to find the subtopics. In this case, each subtopic would be a way in which robots have improved or may improve humans' lives. Skim the article to find where the author discusses these ways. Fill in the subtopic circles with ways in which robots have improved humans' lives and will do so in the future.

3. Now look for details about each subtopic. These go in the box under the subtopic. For example, under the subtopic "work in factories," you might list "relieve humans from tedious or dangerous jobs" and "first happened in the 1960s" as details. Fill in all the detail boxes.

Now that you have filled in the **Main Idea Map,** use it to answer the essay question at the top of the page. Write your answer on a separate sheet of paper.

ANSWER Students should indicate that the purpose robots have in common is to make humans' lives better by working in factories and providing everyday convenience and medical convenience. They should then have elaborated with details from the article. For example, one day there may be a robotic nurse that recognizes when a hospital patient is in pain and can then find the patient's doctor. Standards 1,3,4,5,6,7

Turn the Lock

This question asks you to summarize what you have read by identifying the main idea and supporting details. This is an interpretive question. Put together different pieces of the selection to determine its meaning.

Start your essay by stating the main idea. Then give the subtopics and details from the graphic organizer.

Speak Out

You have read about how robots may be used in the future. Think of some ways not mentioned in the article that robots could make your life and other people's lives easier. Prepare a short speech explaining your ideas. Then give your speech to the class.

DIRECTIONS: Read the following story about a girl named Dee who figures out what one of her classmates needs. Then you will use a Story Map. It will help you explain how Dee changes from the beginning of the story to the end.

Everything But a Friend

"Dee?" Mrs. Chan, my fifth-grade teacher, called on me to answer a question about a story she was reading to the class. I didn't hear what she asked because I was too busy watching Lionel Camacho sleeping while sitting up just two rows from me.

"Uhm," I replied. I couldn't think of a thing to say, but Cassy, the girl who sits in front of me, sure could. She turned around and scowled. Then she primly raised her hand and answered Mrs. Chan's question.

Cassy is very good at everything and I think she knows it. She won the hundred-yard dash on Field Day last month even though she's small for her age. She has pretty blonde hair and she's very smart, but no one seems to like her very much. It's not too hard to figure out why.

At recess we played flag tag, even Cassy. Mrs. Chan gave Lionel the flag so he could start the game. He beamed as he immediately dropped it right behind Cassy and then took off running.

They ran around and around the circle, but fast as Cassy was she couldn't catch Lionel. The whole time everyone was cheering for Lionel and laughing at Cassy. Her face got red and she clenched her teeth as she slowly gave up the chase. Finally, she stopped running and pushed the kid standing closest to her. That kid happened to be me! What a *mess*—that was what Mrs. Chan called it. Then she told us we'd just lost our recess for the next day. The class glared at Cassy. *Nobody* liked her.

That night I told my parents what happened.

"Cassy is the worst! She's such a snob! Everybody hates her. And she pushed me yesterday at recess."

"You mean that little O'Reilly girl? The one who's no bigger than a minute?" Mom asked.

"Yes, her. She also won the hundred-yard dash on Field Day. And she knows the answers to all the questions, and she never does anything fun," I said as I rolled my eyes.

"What about friends, Dee?" Dad asked. "It doesn't sound like Cassy has too many friends. You think she'd be different if she had one?"

Mom and Dad looked at each other. I knew what they were getting at. But there was no way I was going to put myself in that situation! Everyone would end up hating me, too, if I were to try to become friends with Cassy.

But on the bus ride to school the next day, I kept thinking about what Dad said. What would Cassy be like if she had friends? Was it even possible? I wondered how I would act if I didn't have friends. Against my better judgment, I allowed myself to feel a little bad about the nasty things I had said about her.

Cassy was leaning against the building waiting for the bell when I got off the bus. Still thinking about what it would be like if I didn't have any friends, I walked past her. From out of nowhere, I smiled and said hi. I think both of us looked shocked as I walked by. What was I thinking?!

Later in the day, Mrs. Chan made Carl and me captains for a spelling bee. Lionel was the first person Carl picked. Then everyone except Cassy turned and looked anxiously to see who I would pick first. Cassy was looking at the floor. All of a sudden I felt really sorry for her, and it was all my parents' fault! I probably wouldn't have any friends because of what I was about to do.

"I pick Cassy," I heard myself say. But Cassy didn't budge. Mrs. Chan had to tell her, "Cassy, go stand next to Dee." Cassy seemed to wake up and then quickly joined me. I looked around to see if I was getting any death stares. It didn't look like it, but some kids definitely looked surprised. Feeling a little better about things, I whispered to Cassy that she could pick the next person for our team.

Now we're in sixth grade and tomorrow is Cassy's birthday. She invited me and a couple of other girls to her pizza party and sleepover. She's definitely loosened up a little. Sometimes she even tells a joke or two. The funny thing is, when I look back on that moment I picked Cassy to be on my team, I think about two things. The first is that I learned something new and surprising about someone else. But more importantly, I learned something new and surprising about myself.

Story Map

A **Story Map** helps you understand a story by listing the different parts of the story. In this organizer, there is a box for the different parts of the story you just read about. Fill in each box with details from the story.

Read the essay question and instructions on page 41.

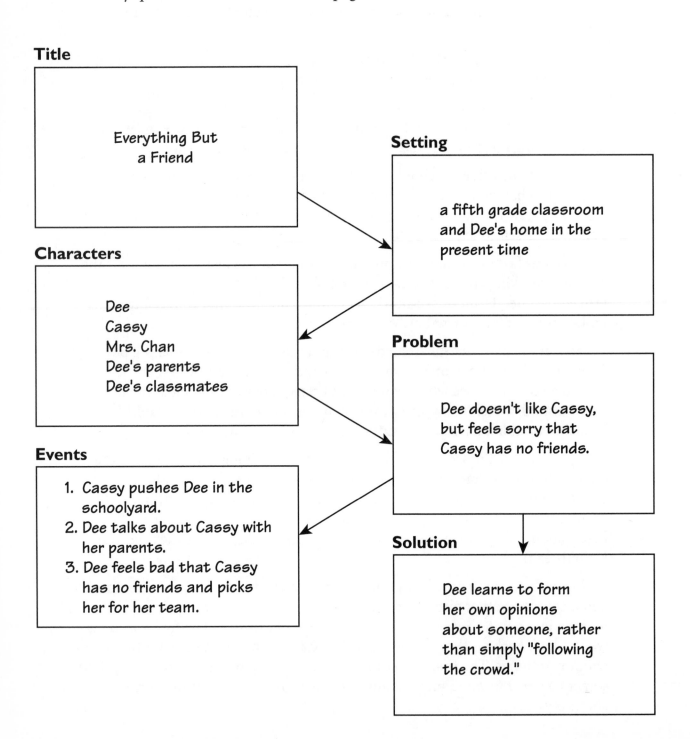

Title

Everything But
a Friend

Setting

a fifth grade classroom
and Dee's home in the
present time

Characters

Dee
Cassy
Mrs. Chan
Dee's parents
Dee's classmates

Problem

Dee doesn't like Cassy,
but feels sorry that
Cassy has no friends.

Events

1. Cassy pushes Dee in the
   schoolyard.
2. Dee talks about Cassy with
   her parents.
3. Dee feels bad that Cassy
   has no friends and picks
   her for her team.

Solution

Dee learns to form
her own opinions
about someone, rather
than simply "following
the crowd."

Essay Question: How does Dee change throughout the story? Why do you think she changes? Be sure to use examples and details from the story.

1. Start by filling in the first three boxes for the *Title, Setting* (there may be more than one setting in the story), and *Characters*. Write "main" next to the name of each of the most important characters.

2. For the fourth box, think about the *main* problem in the story. We know that Cassy has a problem. But consider Dee's problem as the *main* problem. What problem is Dee having at school? Write it in the box.

3. The next box is for the main events that happen in the story. List them in order and number each one. Then, in the last box, write how Dee's problem is solved.

Now that you have filled in the **Story Map,** use it to answer the essay question at the top of the page. Write your answer on a separate sheet of paper.

ANSWER Answers will vary. Students should provide a description of Dee from the early part of the story and a description from the end of the story. Each description should include details from the story. Students may say that Dee followed what her classmates did in the beginning of the story, but learned to make her own decisions by the end of the story. The change should be consistent with the problem/solution presented on the Story Map. Standards 1,3,4,5,6,7,11

Open the Door

This question asks you to evaluate the meaning of the passage by listing some details about the story. This is a critical question. You must look back at the story for clues, but you must also go beyond the text and use your judgment.

Look at the **Story Map.** This information will guide you in writing about the story's events and how Dee has changed. You need to think carefully about the story. Consider how Dee feels in the beginning of the story and what her main problem is. Then look at what happens in the story and how Dee solves her problem. How does this change her as a person?

DIRECTIONS: Read the following poem about a woman who likes to clean too much. Then you will use a Sequence Map. It will help you explain what happens to the woman in the poem.

Going Too Far

by Mildred Howells

A woman who lived in Holland, of old,

Polished her brass till it shone like gold.

She washed her pig after all his meals

In spite of his energetic squeals.

She scrubbed her doorstep into the ground,

And the children's faces, pink and round,

She washed so hard that in several cases

She polished their features off their faces—

Which gave them an odd appearance, though

She thought they were really neater so!

Then her passion for cleaning quickly grew,

And she scrubbed and polished the village through,

Until, to the rage of all the people,

She cleaned the weather-vane off the steeple.

As she looked at the sky one summer's night
She thought that the stars shone out less bright;
And she said with a sigh, "If I were there,
I'd rub them up till the world should stare."
That night a storm began to brew,
And a wind from the ocean blew and blew
Till, when she came to her door next day
It whisked her up, and blew her away—
Up and up in the air so high
That she vanished, at last, in the stormy sky.
Since then it's said that each twinkling star
And the big white moon shine brighter far.
But the neighbors shake their heads in fear
She may rub so hard they will disappear!

Sequence Map

Sequence is the order in which events happen. A **Sequence Map** shows you the order of the events in a story. In this organizer, there is a group of boxes joined by arrows. The first event goes in the first box, the second event goes in the second box, and so on. You can use as many boxes as you need. Next to each box is an oval. Here you write the details about each event.

Read the essay question and instructions on page 45.

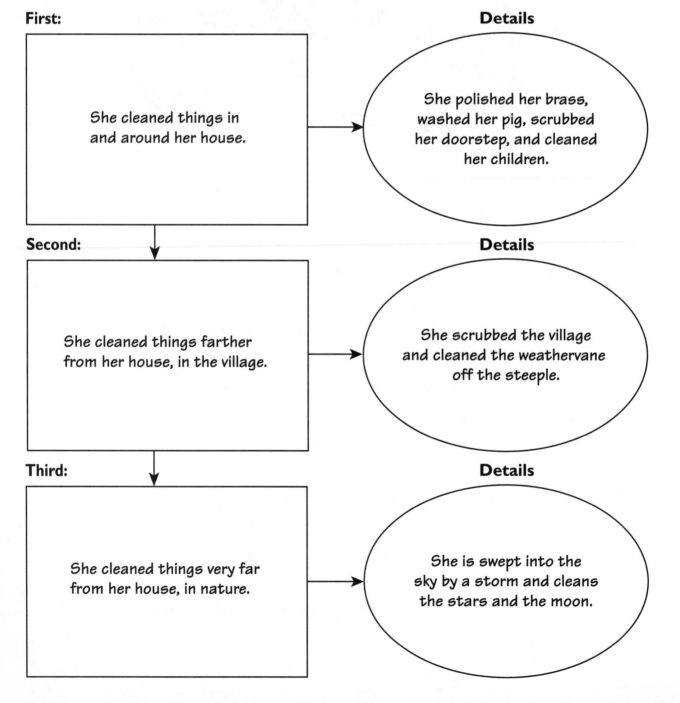

First:

She cleaned things in and around her house.

Details

She polished her brass, washed her pig, scrubbed her doorstep, and cleaned her children.

Second:

She cleaned things farther from her house, in the village.

Details

She scrubbed the village and cleaned the weathervane off the steeple.

Third:

She cleaned things very far from her house, in nature.

Details

She is swept into the sky by a storm and cleans the stars and the moon.

This page may not be reproduced without permission of Steck-Vaughn/Berrent.

Essay Question: How did the woman go from cleaning usual things like brass objects to cleaning the moon? Use details from the poem to trace the sequence.

1. The graphic organizer will help you put the poem's events in order. Skim the poem. Think of the sequence of events in terms of the categories of objects the woman wanted to clean. She started by cleaning things and people at her own home. Write this event in the first box. Then write the details of the event in the oval next to the box.

2. Next, she cleaned things in the village. This is the second event. Write it in the second box. Then write the details of this event in the oval next to it.

3. Finally, she wanted to clean things in nature. Write the event in the third box. Then write the details in the oval next to the box.

Now that you have filled in the **Sequence Map,** use it to answer the essay question at the top of the page. Write your answer on a separate sheet of paper.

ANSWER Answers will vary. Students should elaborate on the categories of objects the woman cleaned or wanted to clean and the details they mentioned in their Sequence Map. The idea that the woman wanted to clean things that were increasingly farther from her house and wanted to clean on an ever-larger scale should be made apparent. Standards 1,2,3,4,5,6,7

Turn the Lock

This question asks you to summarize the story by listing the order of events in the story. This is an interpretive question. You must put together different pieces of the selection.

Look at the graphic organizer. Use what you listed to write your essay. In your answer, mention the categories of objects the woman wanted to clean, as well as the details you included in the graphic organizer.

DIRECTIONS: Read the following article about a woman's efforts to help the environment. Then you will use a Cause and Effect Map. It will help you write a letter about this woman and her accomplishments.

The Ocean Is Not a Dump!

by Claudia Atticot

Saving the New Jersey Shore One Beach at a Time

When she was just a little girl watching *National Geographic* specials on television, Cindy Zipf dreamed she would someday be a marine biologist. She spent most of her free time at the beaches in Rumson, New Jersey, where she grew up. "I was always happiest when I was in the water," she says.

Her dream came true. As a young scientist, Zipf worked at a marine biology lab. Part of her job was to study fish that had been exposed to toxins. She was horrified to see how fish jumped out of their tanks in reaction to the poison. Right then, she took up the fight to protect the sea creatures of the Atlantic Ocean from the deadly effects of chemical pollution.

Waves of Poison

In 1984, Zipf started Clean Ocean Action in a spare bedroom of her apartment over a hardware store in Sea Bright, New Jersey. The group's target: the Jersey Shore, which was known as the ocean-dumping capital of the world. There were a whopping eight legal toxic-waste dump sites along its coastline! "The ocean is the perfect dump site because it's open all the time and it's free. So no one really knew what was going on," Zipf explains. Offshore was a toxic stain that covered about 56 square miles!

It took about a year of gathering petitions, writing letters, protesting and organizing rallies to stop the dumping. Gabriella Kelly, 11, who nominated Zipf as a Hometown Hero, helped with the beach cleanups, letters of protest and marches. She even spoke out at a public hearing. Finally, on September 1, 1997, the last dump site was closed. It felt like a big victory!

Sadly, just two years later, Zipf found out that some companies which had permission to dump waste that was safe for the ocean were also dumping chemicals that caused a lot more damage.

Last summer Zipf, 43, brought national attention to the new troubles by walking from Cape May on the southern tip of New Jersey to a spot called Sandy Hook— a 127-mile trip! The eight-day march was called "Dump No More—March for the Shore" to protest violations of the 1997 agreement.

Before joining the march, citizens of New Jersey sent more than 150,000 signed petitions to Al Gore, who was then Vice President.

"All along the way, people who saw me marching decided to join in to march for the cause," Zipf said. She hopes she can soon shut down Clean Ocean Action. But that won't happen, she says, until the Atlantic Ocean off New Jersey is finally safe.

Cindy Zipf (shown at right) walked 127 miles to protest the dumping of toxic waste along New Jersey's shoreline.

Cause and Effect Map

A *cause* tells you why something happened. An *effect* is what happened as a result. A **Cause and Effect Map** helps you organize causes and effects. In this organizer, there are three pairs of boxes. Each pair is connected with an arrow. The first box in each pair is for a cause. The second box is for its effect. You can add as many boxes as you need.

Read the essay question and instructions on page 49.

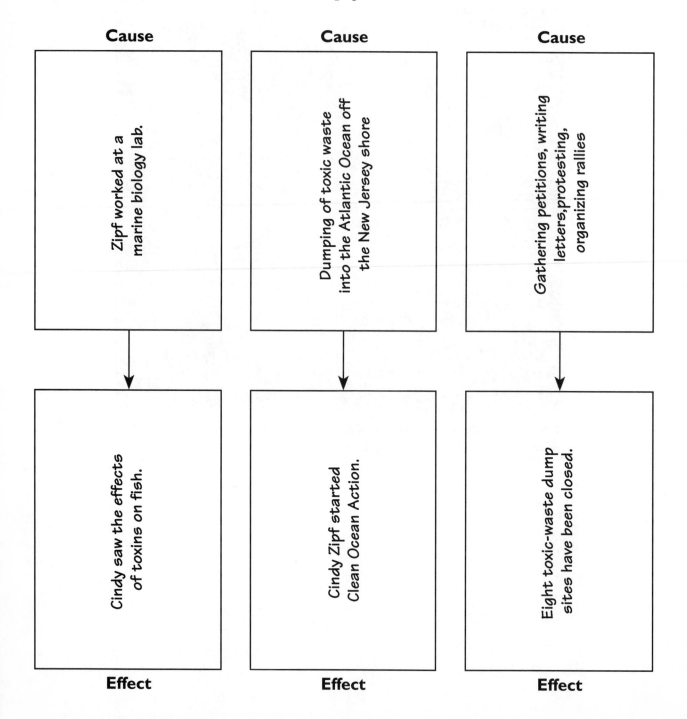

Cause

Zipf worked at a marine biology lab.

Cause

Dumping of toxic waste into the Atlantic Ocean off the New Jersey shore

Cause

Gathering petitions, writing letters, protesting, organizing rallies

Cindy saw the effects of toxins on fish.

Cindy Zipf started Clean Ocean Action.

Eight toxic-waste dump sites have been closed.

Effect   **Effect**   **Effect**

Essay Question: Imagine that you talked to Cindy Zipf and that you were inspired by her work. In a letter to the editor of your town's newspaper, tell why Zipf started Clean Ocean Action and what the organization has achieved.

1. To answer this question, you must know why Cindy Zipf started Clean Ocean Action and what the organization has achieved. Also consider how Zipf became interested in protecting marine wildlife. Look at the first pair of boxes. In the *cause* box on the top write "Zipf worked at a marine biology lab." Then skim the article to find out the effect of this—in other words, what happened because of this. Write the effect in the *effect* box on the bottom.

2. Next, look at the second pair of boxes. In the *effect* box on the bottom, write "Cindy Zipf started Clean Ocean Action." Then skim the article to find out why she started it. Write that cause in the *cause* box on the top.

3. Last, write "Gathering petitions, writing letters, protesting, organizing rallies" in the third *cause* box on the top. Then fill in the effects of these actions in the box on the bottom.

Now that you have filled in the **Cause and Effect Map,** use it to answer the essay question at the top of the page. Write your answer on a separate sheet of paper.

ANSWER Answers will vary. Students should write the letter from the point of view of someone who has met with and been inspired by Cindy Zipf. First, they should mention some background information. For example, they should mention that when Zipf was working in a marine biology lab, she saw the effects of toxins on fish. They should also mention why she started Clean Ocean Action: to stop the dumping of toxic waste into the Atlantic Ocean off the New Jersey shore. Then, they should describe the effects of Clean Ocean Action's actions: the closing of eight toxic-waste dump sites.   Standards 1,3,4,5,6,7,12

Turn the Lock

This is a cause-and-effect question in which you must identify details from the article. This is an interpretive question. You must put together different pieces of the selection to determine its meaning.

Now use the graphic organizer to help you write your letter. Write as if you were someone who had talked with and been inspired by Cindy Zipf. First, write about why Zipf started the organization. Then, write about what the organization has achieved.

DIRECTIONS: Read the following story about a girl who learns some surprising facts about her past. Then you will use a Venn Diagram. It will help you compare the girl's present to her past.

A Free Ride

by Rebecca Aberg

"Tell me, Father, how did we escape and come to America?" Chua had only been three years old then, and she wanted to hear the story that went with the flash of jungle and river in her memory. Usually, her father would just look away when she asked. But today the house was quiet. The rest of the family was gone, and she hoped that he'd tell her. They sat on the floor, side by side in a patch of sunlight.

Father sighed. "In Laos there was no time, no time to get ready. The Vietnam War had ended. Messengers came and told us that **Pathet Lao** soldiers were coming toward our village. Soldiers who had killed your grandfather and uncle and who would kill us if we stayed, because we fought against them during the war." Chua's father talked slowly. She sat close to him, hugging her knees and looking up at his face, but her father's eyes looked past her, through the open window.

Pathet Lao = North Vietnamese Communist soldiers

He continued in his soft, deep voice. "We had to leave everything, because it was a long journey to Thailand, where we'd be safe. At night, in the dark, we left our home."

"We were brave, weren't we, Father?"

Chua's father turned and looked down into her dark eyes. "Yes, Chua, we had to be brave and strong. You were brave. You could not make a sound or cry, even though you became weak and hungry as we walked and walked through the jungle. We heard tigers in the brush and the screams of the monkeys. We had no fire to comfort us. We could not rest. Then on the twelfth night we came to a river."

"The Mekong?"

"Yes. And what do you know of this river?"

In her memory, Chua saw the dark swirling water and smelled the dead leaves along the banks, but even more she remembered the taste of fear in her throat. Her mother told her that monsters lived beneath the water. They'd drag you under, for they were very hungry. She turned to her father. "It's deep and wide, and many **Hmong** people died crossing it. Others were captured by soldiers along its banks. On the other side of the Mekong was safety in Thailand."

"That is right, Chua. Your mother and I looked at the dark river, and it was like an angry snake. We did not know how we'd get across. We watched two brothers wade into the water and begin to swim, but it was too dark to see them go far. We knew many people died crossing this way. If we had tried, we wouldn't have made it to the other side. You were too small to swim and too weak to hang on to my shoulders.

"We saw a boat loading people upstream, and I ran to them but was pushed aside. Those people had paid with silver bars, but we had no silver. As the boat pulled away, the people stared back at us. We were left alone on the shore.

"We were lucky there was no moon that night to give the soldiers an eye to see us. Even so we felt their cold fingers on our spines. Time was pushing us to the water. We waited until it was very late, hoping others would come with a raft or boat to help us cross. It was so dark that we could not see each other, but we could hear each other breathing, the beating of our own hearts, the thirsty slap of the river.

"Then suddenly a man grabbed my arm and clamped his hand over my mouth. I struggled to get away, but he spoke a word of Hmong in my ear and led us away from the river. He pushed my hands on something round and smooth hidden in the bushes. It was an inner tube. That man was giving us a

Hmong = an ethnic group in Asia

way to cross the river. I never saw his face, but I will always remember his words. He said, 'I am here to help you. Here is your free ride.'"

Chua looked up from where she'd been tracing the pattern of the grain of the floorboards with her finger. "We crossed in an inner tube?"

"Yes." Her father continued as if this wasn't so unusual. "We put you in the rubber ring, and I swam across towing the tube. Your mother was very brave, and she hung from behind and kicked to help push us through the strong current. Together we made it across."

"Then we were safe and came to America?" Chua asked.

"Not right away. Hmong people helped us find the refugee camp at Ban Vinai; we lived there for almost two years before we could get on an airplane and come to America. It was hard to wait, but it was also hard to leave."

"Why don't you like to tell this story, Father? It's a good story."

"We must look forward, not backward." He smiled at Chua and brushed her cheek lightly with the back of his hand.

Chua went outside, blinking in the bright summer light, still feeling her father's touch on her cheek. Today she was meeting friends at the public pool. She felt her long hair sway lightly on her back as she walked. It was hard to imagine that they'd really escaped from Laos ten years earlier. It seemed so long ago, like another life. Like her father, she wouldn't think of it again, she told herself, and she began to run.

Later, she and her friends sat drying on their towels, enjoying the smells and taste of soda and hot nachos. They talked about school and teachers, boys they liked and boys they didn't like. After a while they fell quiet, feeling the sun warm their backs and watching other swimmers.

A little girl caught Chua's attention. The girl's father was pulling her through the bright water on a small inner tube. She couldn't take her eyes away from the child and the tiny fingers that clung to the plastic ring. She imagined herself and her own father. Again she heard his softly spoken words, "We had to be brave and strong. You were brave."

"What are you looking at?" Emily asked.

Chua turned to face her friend, realizing she'd been caught daydreaming. Crunching loudly on a chip, Emily waited for her to answer. Chua paused, trying to think of what to say. She studied the bright flowers on Emily's swimsuit. How could she explain that she was remembering the fear in the jungle, the danger that waited by the river, the feeling of sadness and joy that mixed together when she thought about leaving Laos? She looked into Emily's blue eyes knowing she'd never be able to explain.

"I'm looking at a girl getting a free ride," she said finally and offered Emily one of her chips.

Venn Diagram

A **Venn Diagram** helps you describe how two things are alike and how they are different. In this organizer, there are two overlapping ovals. The name of each of the things being compared goes at the top of each oval. The ways the two things are different go in the *outside* parts of the ovals, the parts that do not overlap. The ways they are alike go in the middle *overlapping* part.

Read the essay question and instructions on page 55.

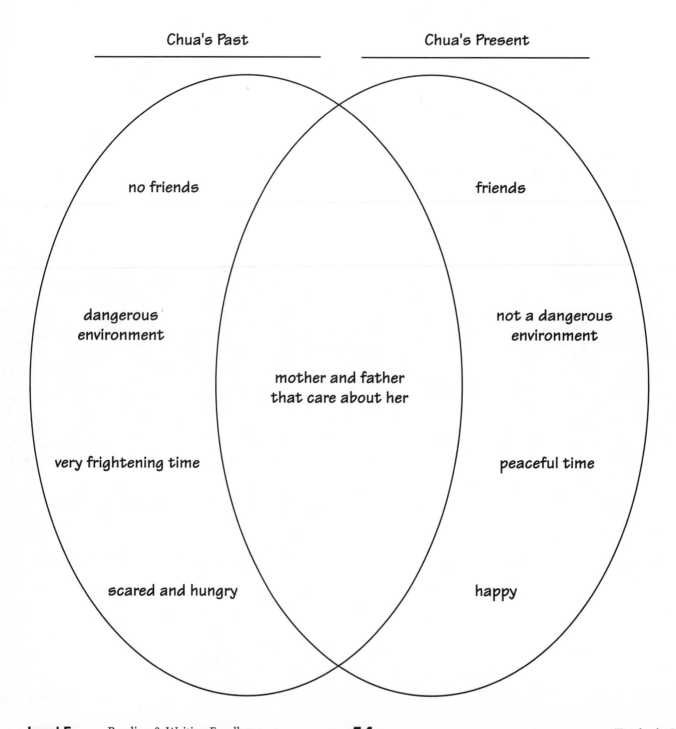

Chua's Past

Chua's Present

no friends

friends

dangerous environment

not a dangerous environment

mother and father that care about her

very frightening time

peaceful time

scared and hungry

happy

Essay Question: Think about Chua's past, as she was escaping from Laos, and her present, when she is at the pool with her friends. What about her past and present is similar? What is different?

1. You will be comparing Chua's past, when she was escaping from Laos, to her present, when she is at the pool. Write "Chua's Past" at the top of the first oval. At the top of the second oval, write "Chua's Present."

2. Next, scan through the story for clues to tell you about Chua's past. Write the ways that her past is different from her present in the outside part of the first oval. Then write how Chua's present is different from her past in the outside part of the second oval.

3. Now think about how Chua's past and present are alike. Is there anything about Chua's life that has remained the same over time? Write these details in the middle *overlapping* part of the ovals.

Now that you have filled in the **Venn Diagram,** use it to answer the essay question at the top of the page. Write your answer on a separate sheet of paper.

ANSWER Answers will vary. In describing Chua's past, students might mention that Chua had no friends but did have her mother and father; that the environment she was in was full of danger; and that she probably felt very scared and hungry. Then students might mention that in Chua's present, she is still with her mother and father and that she also has friends; that the environment holds no danger but instead is pleasant; and that she probably feels thankful and happy to be where she is.   Standards 1,2,3,4,5,6,7,9

Turn the Lock

Here you must compare and contrast information about Chua's past and her present. To do this, you must identify details from the story. This is an interpretive question. You must gather details and reach a conclusion about these details.

Look at the graphic organizer. Use what you listed to write your essay. Write about Chua's past and her present. Then try to reach a conclusion about Chua. How has her past affected her present life?

After You Write

Use this list to check your writing.

Revise:

☐ Did you answer the question?

☐ Did you stay on the topic?

☐ Is there an opening and a closing?

☐ Did you support your main ideas with details?

☐ Did you organize your ideas clearly?

☐ Did you vary your words and sentences?

☐ Do all the words make sense?

☐ Is your writing interesting?

☐ Is your writing easy to read?

Edit:

☐ Do verbs agree with their subjects?

☐ Are pronouns used correctly?

☐ Are the spelling, capitalization, and punctuation correct?

Summary

You can use graphic organizers to help you recall and understand what you have read. Graphic organizers can also help you answer essay questions about a selection. They help you put your ideas and thoughts in order before you begin to write.

In this unit, you have learned about the following graphic organizers:

 **Character Traits Web**

 **Sequence Map**

 Main Idea Map

 Cause and Effect Map

 **Story Map**

 **Venn Diagram**

 **4Rs** Remember that when answering an essay question, you should always use the **Four Rs**: **R**eady, **R**ead, **R**espond, **R**eview. When you review your work, use a checklist such as the one above.

UNIT 3
Introduction—
Guided Practice

The previous units have taught all the skills necessary to succeed in testing situations. Students have learned the **Four *R*s** strategy, have discovered how to answer questions at the three levels of comprehension (literal, interpretive, and critical), and have acquired strategies for approaching multiple-choice and open-ended questions. They have also studied how graphic organizers can arrange information to help them answer essay questions.

Unit 3 builds upon what was taught in the previous units. Students apply what they have learned by taking a practice test that includes six reading selections from various genres. The last two passages, which are linked, are followed by one set of questions. The questions on the practice test represent the three levels of comprehension. In addition, each question includes a hint to help students respond. For each essay question, the hint suggests which graphic organizer would best aid students in organizing their thoughts.

The purpose of this practice test is to prepare students for an actual testing situation while still providing some guidance. This test will serve to accomplish four goals:

▶ ***To increase awareness of directions***—It is important that students understand the directions for taking a test. Familiarizing them with directions will build self-confidence and permit them to utilize their time more efficiently.

▶ ***To increase awareness of content and skills***—Anxiety often results from a lack of information about the knowledge and skills the test will cover. Increased awareness of content and skills will help students meet with optimal success in an actual testing situation.

▶ ***To increase awareness of format***—By practicing the skills needed, students will gain invaluable experience with test formats. Such familiarity permits students to spend more time applying what they have learned.

▶ ***To increase awareness of how a test is administered***—Students are sometimes uncomfortable anticipating what will happen on a testing day. Becoming familiar with the procedures, directions, and the process of test taking helps reduce anxiety and uncertainty.

You may choose either to work through the test with students or to simulate a test situation without grading the students on their performance. If you choose to work with the students, encourage them first to use the hint to answer the question on their own. You may then provide additional assistance if it is required.

If you wish, you might also allow students to work together in small groups. Small group work provides an opportunity for students to develop cooperative attitudes and group decision-making skills. It allows them to become active agents in the testing process by encouraging them to bring ideas to the attention of others in a comfortable group atmosphere. Such an activity will decrease the anxiety students might feel during an independent testing situation.

If the students are completing the test independently, go over the Test-Taking Guidelines on page 89A of this guide with the class before they begin. It will also be important for you to keep in touch with each student's progress. If a student is having a great deal of difficulty, you might want to offer assistance during the test. After the test, go over the answers with the class. Be sure that students realize why they missed any answers and provide additional instruction if necessary.

If you choose to, you may test your students' listening skills by reading them the passage on pages 64-65 and the poem on page 77 of the Student Book. These two selections are simple enough in plot that they lend themselves well to being used in listening situations. Do not allow the students to view these selections while you read them aloud, but have the students answer the questions on the pages following the selections as they do with the other passages in the book.

Finally, you will note that it is here, in Unit 3, that the third and final "Speak Out" will be found. It is recommended that you give your students the opportunity to utilize this final "Speak Out," in order to obtain a greater degree of comfort and confidence in their public speaking skills.

The following pages are picked up from Unit 3 in the Student Book for Level E. The correct answers to the multiple-choice questions have been filled in at the bottom of the page, possible answers to the short-answer questions have been added, possible completions of the graphic organizers have been included, and requirements for the essay answers have been given.

Guided Practice

Now you are going to practice what you have learned by reading several selections. You will be asked to answer multiple-choice, short-answer, and essay questions about what you have read. These questions will be at the three key levels of comprehension: literal, interpretive, and critical. You will be given a hint to help you answer each question.

Regardless of what type of selection you read or question you answer, you should always follow the **Four *R*s:**

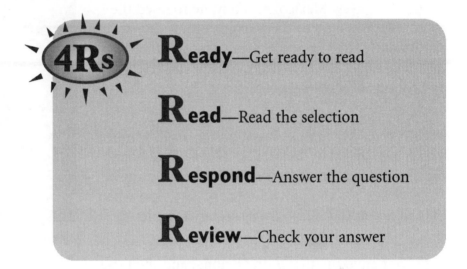

4Rs

Ready—Get ready to read

Read—Read the selection

Respond—Answer the question

Review—Check your answer

DIRECTIONS: Read this article about an amazing artist. Then answer questions 1 through 6. Darken the circle at the bottom of the page or write your answer on the lines.

A Touch of Genius

by Patricia Millman

Michael Naranjo is a Native American, a Vietnam War veteran, and "a sculptor who happens to be blind." Behind this statement lies a remarkable story.

Michael grew up in the Tewa Indian **pueblo** of Santa Clara, New Mexico. As a boy, he roamed the scenic foothills west of the pueblo community and explored the Rio Grande, a river to the south and east. His world was enriched by the beautiful sights and sounds of the desert country.

Michael's love of sculpting was born at the pueblo, too. "My mother was a potter, and I would help her fix her clay," he recalls. "She gathered her clay in a place in the hills that only she knew about. Every potter has their own source of clay. And when they find that clay, they're very secretive about it.

Michael Naranjo shown at left with his sculpture "Spirit Soaring."

"My mother would bring in the clay and screen it to get out anything that didn't belong, and then she would soak it in tubs. After that, she'd put the clay into a square of canvas cloth, and she'd sprinkle a different white kind of clay on top. Then she would fold this square of canvas and press on it this way and that way, and when she unfolded the canvas I could see this little log of clay inside.

"Then I would take off my shoes and perform a little dance with the clay. I would sidestep on this log of clay. I could feel the moist clay on the side of my foot and between my toes. And when I reached the other end, I'd step off the square of canvas, and she'd fold it and push it this way and that way and refold it, and I would have this little log of clay again. And once again I would perform my little dance."

Michael's dance served a very important purpose. He was blending the white clay and the brown clay to make it stronger. With this strong clay, his mother could make pots that would last a long time.

pueblo = a communal village of some Native Americans of the Southwest United States

"That's probably how I started sculpting . . . playing with clay," Michael says. "Not long after that, I wanted to make figures of animals. And as they became more detailed, they became sculptures. So even way back then, I knew that what I wanted to do was be an artist someday."

Seeing with His Hands

Michael's goal would not be reached easily. While serving with the Army in Vietnam, Michael was badly wounded in battle. He lost his sight and partial use of one hand. For the first time, Michael wondered if he could ever be a sculptor.

One day, while recovering in the hospital, Michael asked if he could have a small piece of clay. From it he made an inchworm.

The next sculpture Michael made, an Indian on a horse, was so good it was photographed by the newspapers. Lucky thing! Because when Michael decided to make his next sculpture, he found that the hospital didn't have any more clay. So he reshaped the Indian on a horse into a bear with a fish in its mouth.

Today, Michael has lots of material to use to make his memories come to life. "I was able to see until I was twenty-three years old. So I have a very good idea of what most things look like," he said. "So I sit, and I think about it, and I get a picture in my mind. If you close your eyes and think of . . . well, if you have a cat or a dog, you can picture this pet. The same process happens with me.

"Once you have the material in your hand that you can mold and shape, then you can carry it over from your mind to your fingertips. And your mind tells your fingers, 'Make that bigger or smaller . . .' until this whole process slowly starts happening.

"Nowadays, when I make animals, I sit there and think about the days when I'd take a moment sitting on a cliff side and look down and see a deer down there or watch some turkeys walk through the forest. Or the time I followed a mountain stream and a deer stopped in this pool of water and looked at me with his huge, brown eyes. It lasted just a few moments, but it's one of those moments that I draw on for inspiration."

Michael inspires others by leading sculpture workshops for children and adults, veterans and seniors, both sighted and visually impaired.

In 1999, Michael was named the Outstanding Disabled Veteran of the Year. He also received the LIFE Presidential Unsung Hero Award. His sculptures can be seen in museums and public buildings across the United States, in the Vatican, and in the White House.

Does Michael have one piece of sculpture that is his favorite? Could it be the buffalo from the Santa Fe Indian Market? Or the bear with a fish in its mouth?

"You know, it's the same as with children," Michael said. "If you have more than one, you love them all equally. That's how I feel about my sculptures."

1 For Michael, figures of animals became sculptures—

 A when he was old enough to play with the clay

 B when the correct kind of clay had been used

 C after he added details to the figures

 D after he realized that he had artistic talent

Hint Identify details from the article. You will find the answer to this question right in the selection. Think about where this information might appear. Then use key words in the question to find the answer in the selection.

2 From the article you can conclude that Michael—

 F uses the same kind of clay his mother used

 G would prefer not to lead sculpture workshops

 H still lives in a Tewa Indian pueblo

 J enjoyed helping his mother fix her clay

Hint Draw a conclusion based on what you read. The answer is not directly stated in the selection. You must figure it out. First, eliminate any choice that you know is false. Then, look closely at the choices that are left. Which one is supported by facts stated in the article?

3 Which of the following is an *opinion* from the article?

 A Michael grew up in the Tewa Indian pueblo of Santa Clara, New Mexico.

 B Michael's goal would not be reached easily.

 C He lost his sight and partial use of one hand.

 D In 1999, Michael was named the Outstanding Disabled Veteran of the Year.

Hint Identify an opinion from the article. Remember that a fact is something that is true. An opinion is not necessarily true. It is what someone believes to be true. Which choice sounds like a belief?

Answers

1 Ⓐ Ⓑ ● Ⓓ	2 Ⓕ Ⓖ Ⓗ ●	3 Ⓐ ● Ⓒ Ⓓ
Standards 1,2,3	**Standards 1,2,3**	**Standards 1,2,3,11**

4 At the end of the article, Michael compares sculptures to children. In what way are the two alike?

He says that a parent who has more than one child does not love one more than

the others. For him, his sculptures are like children. So he does not have a favorite

one because he loves them all equally.

Standards 1,2,3,4,5,6

 Hint Identify details. Look for the place in the article where Michael makes this comparison. Answer the question in your own words.

5 Why does Michael Naranjo mention the deer that looked at him with huge, brown eyes?

It is an example of the memories he uses for inspiration.

Standards 1,2,3,4,5,6

 Hint This question requires you to draw a conclusion from information found in the article. Consider how Michael was affected by his experience with the deer. Carefully reread this part of the article. Look for words that explain this experience for Michael.

6 Michael Naranjo is a special artist because of certain events that happened earlier in his life. Describe these events and the impact they had on him.

 A Cause and Effect Map will help you organize information about the most important events that led to Michael Naranjo becoming a special sculptor. Write the events in the "Cause" row of boxes. Write each event's effect, or impact on Michael, in the "Effect" row of boxes.

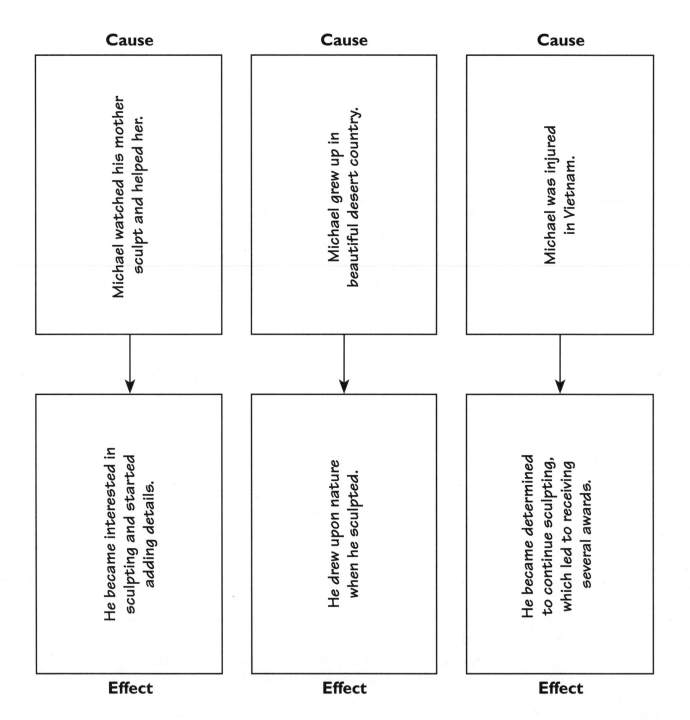

Cause

Michael watched his mother sculpt and helped her.

Cause

Michael grew up in beautiful desert country.

Cause

Michael was injured in Vietnam.

He became interested in sculpting and started adding details.

Effect

He drew upon nature when he sculpted.

Effect

He became determined to continue sculpting, which led to receiving several awards.

Effect

Write your essay on the lines below. If you need more space, continue writing on a separate sheet of paper.

Answers will vary. Students may mention that Michael watched his mother sculpt

when he was a boy and this may have influenced his own sculpting. They may mention

that he grew up in desert country and had an appreciation for nature that he drew

upon later in life when he became a sculptor. His perseverance after he was injured in

Vietnam showed his determination and led to him receiving several awards.

Standards 1,2,3,4,5,6,7

Hint This is a cause-and-effect question in which you must identify details from the article. Look at the information you wrote in the Cause and Effect Map. Use it to write your essay. Describe the events that led to Michael becoming a special artist. After you finish, use the checklist on page 56 to help you review your writing.

Just a Sunday Drive in the Country

by Pete Hendley

You wouldn't think you'd have to worry about a camel on the loose in Ohio.

My wife and daughters and I were on vacation. We were staying at a cottage on the shore of Lake Erie, and we decided to take a drive out into the countryside on our first day there. I was driving. My wife was in the front with me, and the girls were in the back.

It was a beautiful area—green rolling hills, thick with tall corn growing on both sides of the lazy country road. When we saw a sign advertising fresh sweet corn for sale, we decided to check it out.

We drove up a long dirt road and stopped in front of a large, white farmhouse. All around us were tall, old trees.

A farmer came up to the car. I talked to him through my open window, haggling over a price for the corn, our car still running. Once we came to an agreement, he opened up the back door and loaded a sack of corn onto the floor at my daughters' feet. Suddenly, on our right, a camel appeared from among the tall trees.

"Look! Look!" all three of my children screamed at once.

I couldn't believe it.

Then before we could do anything, the camel strolled up and stuck all of his huge, long head right into my wife's half-open window.

Everyone screamed at once.

"He just wants a piece of corn," the farmer said to my girls, who were in the backseat, squealing and screaming with a mixture of terror and glee.

"Give him the corn," I urged. "Give him the corn!"

The camel's head was *gargantuan*, as long and wide as a good-size dog, and it smelled like a wet rug. His lips moved and slopped constantly as he chewed, and his two cavernous nostrils sniffed at everything. When he turned to my wife, stuck out his tongue, and licked her smack on the face, it was more than my daughters could stand. They screamed and laughed so loud it scared the camel half to death.

He decided he would be better off somewhere else, without his head stuck in such a noisy, impolite box. He tried to pull himself out in one swift motion, but instead he got stuck in the small space created by the half-open window.

That didn't stop him, though. In terror, he yanked with all his camel strength, and amidst all the noise and confusion and panic, the window shattered, sending a shower of glass all over everyone in the car and causing complete and total pandemonium as three panicked children began to rock and bounce in their futile attempts to unbuckle their seat belts and run away.

"Go. Just drive!" my wife yelled. "Get us out of here!" A chorus of tiny voices behind me agreed.

And drive I did, backward, out the way we'd come, the perplexed and friendly farmer scratching his head and apologizing as we went. "He's just a little insistent," the man shouted. "Sorry."

We never did figure out what the camel was doing there.

7 In this story, the word *gargantuan* means—

F straight   H silly

G huge   J skinny

 Hint This is a vocabulary question. The answer is in the story. Find the sentence with the word *gargantuan*. Which choice matches the description in the sentence?

8 In a retelling of the story, which of these would be *least* important?

A The event happened on the family's first day of vacation.

B The family stopped at a farmhouse.

C The farmer put the sack of corn on the back floorboard.

D The camel's head was about the size of a dog.

 Hint Here you must determine which information is not important, or relevant. Which of the choices would a listener need *least* to understand what happened in the story?

9 When the narrator says that "the camel's head . . . smelled like a wet rug," he is using which of the following?

F hyperbole   H simile

G personification   J metaphor

 Hint This question is about vocabulary and what words mean. Hyperbole is exaggeration for effect. Personification gives human qualities to something that is not human. A simile compares two unlike things using *like* or *as*. A metaphor speaks of one thing as if it were something else.

Answers

7 ⓕ ● ⓗ ⓙ	8 ● ⓑ ⓒ ⓓ	9 ⓕ ⓖ ● ⓙ
Standards 1,3,6	**Standards 1,3,11**	**Standards 1,3**

10 The mood of the story suddenly changes in the paragraph that begins with "That didn't stop him, though." How does it change?

Answers should include that the story goes from funny to scary. The author

describes a frightening moment.

Standards 1,3,4,5,6

Hint The mood of the story is how it makes you feel. Describe the mood of the story. Carefully reread this paragraph and a few paragraphs that come before it and after it. Think about the events and what the characters do.

11 At the end of the story, the author says that the farmer was perplexed, or confused. Why was the farmer confused?

The farmer was used to the camel. It did not seem out of the ordinary to him for

the camel to want to eat the corn that was in the car. He could not figure out why

the people in the car were screaming and panicked.

Standards 1,3,4,5,6

Hint Here you must understand what certain things mean in the story, based on the information you are given. Think about the events of the story from the farmer's point of view.

12 Describe how the girls' reaction to the camel changed over the course of the story. Use details from the story to support your answer.

 Reread the story and keep track of the children's reactions. Use a Sequence Map to note the events that took place. Write an event in each box in the order in which they happened. The oval to the right of each box is for the details about that event and how the girls reacted.

First: **Details**

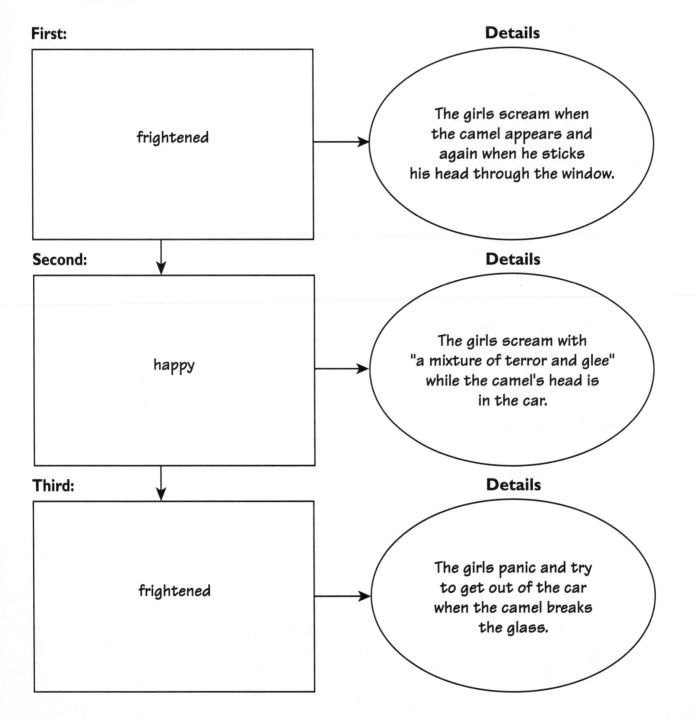

| frightened | → | The girls scream when the camel appears and again when he sticks his head through the window. |

Second: **Details**

| happy | → | The girls scream with "a mixture of terror and glee" while the camel's head is in the car. |

Third: **Details**

| frightened | → | The girls panic and try to get out of the car when the camel breaks the glass. |

Write your essay on the lines below. If you need more space, continue writing on a separate sheet of paper.

Students should mention that the girls screamed when they first saw the camel and

again when it first put its head in the window. But their screams soon became a

"mixture of terror and glee." They were screaming and laughing at the same time when

the animal licked their mother's face. However, their glee and laughter disappeared when

the camel broke the window. Students should support their answer with details from

the story.

Standards 1,3,4,5,6,7

_____

_____

_____

_____

_____

_____

_____

_____

_____

_____

Hint Summarize the girls' reactions by listing the order of events. Look at the information you wrote in your Sequence Map. Use it to write your essay answer. Describe each event in the story and how the girls react to it. Make sure you describe how their reactions change throughout the story. After you finish, remember to use the checklist on page 56 to help you review your writing.

DIRECTIONS: Read this article about an amazing type of seabird. Then answer questions 13 through 18. Darken the circle at the bottom of the page or write your answer on the lines.

Tracking the Wandering Albatross

by Jack Myers

The wandering albatross is a famous and mysterious bird that few of us ever see. Its fame began with sea stories in the days of sailing ships. Those few sailors who ventured into the stormy waters of the southern oceans had a story to tell. Their ships might be followed for days, even for weeks, by an albatross gliding close behind.

There have been scientific studies of the wandering albatross as an interesting bird with a special way of life. To start with, it's the largest seabird, weighing about twenty pounds and with a wingspan often more than ten feet. Its long, narrow wings are better for gliding than for flapping.

The wandering albatross also has two tricks that allow it to spend most of its life on the wing. Gliding looks easier than flying. But just holding wings outstretched takes work by a bird's wing muscles. (Just try holding your arms outstretched for a few minutes. Even though you are not doing any useful work, your arm muscles will soon get tired.)

For the albatross, gliding is easy because of a tricky wing design. A sheet of **cartilage** can lock and hold the wing in position so that gliding does not take much work. That's the first trick.

cartilage = a tough, elastic tissue in animals and humans

Uplifting Air

The second trick has to do with ocean winds. Most gliding birds, like hawks and buzzards, are high flyers. They use the upward-blowing air of warm updrafts to keep them in flight.

The wandering albatross is a low flyer, usually skimming along a few feet above the waves. The waves are the key to the second trick. Ocean waves also make waves in the air above them. A wind blowing over the ocean surface has an upward swirl above every wave it passes.

You know about people who have fun using surfboards to ride the big ocean waves that come onto beaches. The wandering albatross is a wind surfer. It rides each little updraft that a wave gives to the wind blowing against it. Each updraft gives the bird enough lift to coast to the updraft of the next wave.

Where Albatrosses Meet

Once every two years, the wandering albatrosses return to the same lonely islands where they were born. The male and female of a pair have a big greeting ceremony and then get to the business of nest building, mating, and egg laying.

Both parents take turns at the forty-day job of incubating the egg. After that comes a 280-day job of feeding the chick. The male and female go out on flights for several days looking for fish and squid to feed the chick. After the chick learns to fly, it goes off on its own lonely wander, and the parents go off on theirs.

Studies on Land and Sea

The wandering albatross has never known predators. It has no fear of people and has been easy to study during its brief home life on land.

But how do you study the albatross during most of its life wandering over the oceans? Two French scientists figured out how to track the birds for long flights during the nesting season.

They put little radio transmitters on several birds. Then they could locate the birds' positions every few hours by using radio receivers on two satellites. Observations from the satellites were sent to computers in France and were used to draw a map of each bird's flight path.

One male made a thirty-three-day, 9,400 mile flight while the female was home incubating an egg. By day, the albatross traveled distances up to 600 miles. At night, flights were much shorter, and the bird often stopped to rest on the water. But it never stopped for longer than a few hours at a time. It lived up to its reputation as a wanderer.

When the Wind Dies

One kind of weather the albatross did not like was a dead calm with no wind at all. Then it would rest, taking only short flights, waiting for the wind to come. That need for wind explains why the wandering albatross lives where it does— only in the southern ocean around Antarctica, the windiest of all the seas.

Satellite tracking has taken away some, but not all, of the mystery from the wandering albatross. We can only wonder how these birds navigate and find their way where there are no signposts or landmarks. How do they travel thousands of miles on **erratic** or even zigzag courses? And how does each find its way home to a tiny speck of an island?

erratic = irregular

13 All of the following statements about the albatross are true *except*—

   A it is the largest seabird

   B gliding is hard for it

   C it returns to where it was born

   D both parents feed their chicks

 Hint Identify details. You can find the answer in the article. Go back and check each choice to see if it is true.

14 What would be another good title for the article?

   F "An Interesting and Still Mysterious Bird"

   G "Satellite Tracking"

   H "Flight Patterns of Albatrosses"

   J "How the Albatross Glides"

Hint This is a main idea question. The title you choose should not be about only part of the article. What is the article *all* about? Knowing the main idea will help you choose a title.

15 Which of these statements from the article is an *opinion*?

   A Gliding looks easier than flying.

   B Its long, narrow wings are better for gliding than for flapping.

   C It lived up to its reputation as a wanderer.

   D We can only wonder how these birds navigate and find their way where there are no signposts or landmarks.

Hint Identify an opinion. Remember, an *opinion* is a statement of someone's belief, judgment, or way of thinking about something. A *fact* is a statement that can be proved true or false.

Answers

13 Ⓐ ● Ⓒ Ⓓ	**14** ● Ⓖ Ⓗ Ⓙ	**15** ● Ⓑ Ⓒ Ⓓ
Standards 1,3	**Standards 1,3**	**Standards 1,3,11**

16 Why does the albatross have no fear of people?

The albatross has no known predators and rarely comes into contact with people,

so it is not afraid of them. It spends most of its time over water.

Standards 1,3,4,5,6

_____

_____

_____

_____

Hint This is a cause-and-effect question. You will find the answer in the article. Find the part that discusses this statement. Read the sentences before and after it.

17 What is the author's purpose in writing this article?

The author is informing the reader about a fascinating bird and explaining new

findings about the bird.

Standards 1,3,4,5,6,11

_____

_____

_____

_____

Hint Determine the author's purpose. What is this article about? Is it trying to teach you something? Is it telling you a story? How do you think the author wants you to react to the article?

18 The author thinks that the wandering albatross is an "interesting bird with a special way of life." Summarize his description of the albatross to prove that this is true.

 Use a Main Idea Map to organize the author's description of the wandering albatross. Your main idea should be how interesting and special these birds are. Flight tricks, flight distances, and care of eggs and chicks help prove this statement about the albatross. Organize the information and give details.

Main Idea

The albatross is an interesting bird
with a special way of life.

Subtopic

flight tricks

Subtopic

flight distances

Subtopic

care of eggs
and chicks

Details

tricky wing design that
makes gliding easy

uses the updrafts of
wind above the waves

Details

can travel for weeks
and cover thousands
of miles

Details

both parents take care
of incubating the egg

go on several-day
flights looking for
food for the chick

Write your summary on the lines below. If you need more space, continue writing on a separate sheet of paper.

Answers will vary. Students should begin the essay with the idea that the wandering

albatross is "interesting" and "special." They should then address each of the following

three subtopics: flight tricks, flight distances, and care of eggs and chicks. Details

from the article about each subtopic should be included.

Standards 1,3,4,5,6,7

_____

_____

_____

_____

_____

_____

_____

_____

Hint This question asks you to describe the main idea of the article, using supporting details. Use the information on the Main Idea Map to write your summary. State the main idea in your own words, then follow this with information about your first subtopic. Write a paragraph for each of the other two subtopics. Be sure you give plenty of details about each subtopic. Remember to use the checklist on page 56 to review your writing.

DIRECTIONS: Read this poem about Harriet Tubman, the most famous conductor of the Underground Railroad. Conductors on this railroad led enslaved people in the American South who were escaping north to freedom. After you read the poem, answer questions 19 through 24. Darken the circle at the bottom of the page or write your answer on the lines.

Harriet Tubman

by Eloise Greenfield

Harriet Tubman didn't take no stuff
Wasn't scared of nothing neither
Didn't come in this world to be no slave
And wasn't going to stay one either

"Farewell!" she sang to her friends one night
She was mighty sad to leave 'em
But she ran away that dark, hot night
Ran looking for her freedom

She ran to the woods and she ran through the woods
With the slave catchers right behind her
And she kept on going till she got to the North
Where those mean men couldn't find her

Nineteen times she went back South
To get three hundred others
She ran for her freedom nineteen times
To save black sisters and brothers

Harriet Tubman didn't take no stuff
Wasn't scared of nothing neither
Didn't come in this world to be no slave
And didn't stay one either

And didn't stay one either

19 Which of these is *least* important to the meaning of the poem?

    F Harriet Tubman made nineteen trips to the South after she first went north.

    G Slave catchers were trying to capture Harriet Tubman.

    H Harriet Tubman was a strong woman who refused to remain a slave.

    J The night when Harriet Tubman left home was dark and hot.

> **Hint** Determine which information is not important. First decide what the meaning of the poem is. Then think about which choice is not necessary to explain this meaning.

20 Harriet Tubman returned to the South many times to—

    A visit her family

    B win her freedom

    C rescue others from slavery

    D show that she was not afraid

> **Hint** Identify details from the poem. The answer is right in the poem. Reread it carefully. Look for when she returned to the South.

21 The author *most* likely wrote the poem to—

    F inform readers about the Underground Railroad

    G praise Harriet Tubman's actions

    H describe what life was like in the South

    J convince readers that Harriet Tubman is a national hero

> **Hint** Determine the author's purpose. Eliminate the choices that you know are not correct. Then look closely at the ones that are left. Which one is supported by details in the poem and by the language the poet uses?

Answers

19 Ⓕ Ⓖ Ⓗ ●	20 Ⓐ Ⓑ ● Ⓓ	21 Ⓕ ● Ⓗ Ⓙ
Standards 1,2,3,11	**Standards 1,2,3**	**Standards 1,2,3,11**

22 What is the theme of the poem?

Answers should include words like "determination" and "courage."

Standards 1,2,3,4,5,6

> **Hint** Determine the theme of the poem. What is the message that the poem is trying to send? Look carefully at the language the poet uses as she talks about Harriet Tubman.

23 What is the mood of the poem? Use details from the poem.

The mood of the poem is serious and the speaker expresses pride in Tubman's

accomplishments.

Standards 1,2,3,4,5,6

> **Hint** Determine the mood, or overall feeling of the selection. Often the mood can be described in a few words.

24 It took a very special person to accomplish what Harriet Tubman did. Describe Harriet Tubman and the traits that she possesses. Use details from the poem to support your answer.

 Before you can answer this, you must think about Harriet Tubman's character traits. Fill in a Character Traits Web about her. Use as many boxes for traits as you can. This will help you write your essay answer later.

Character

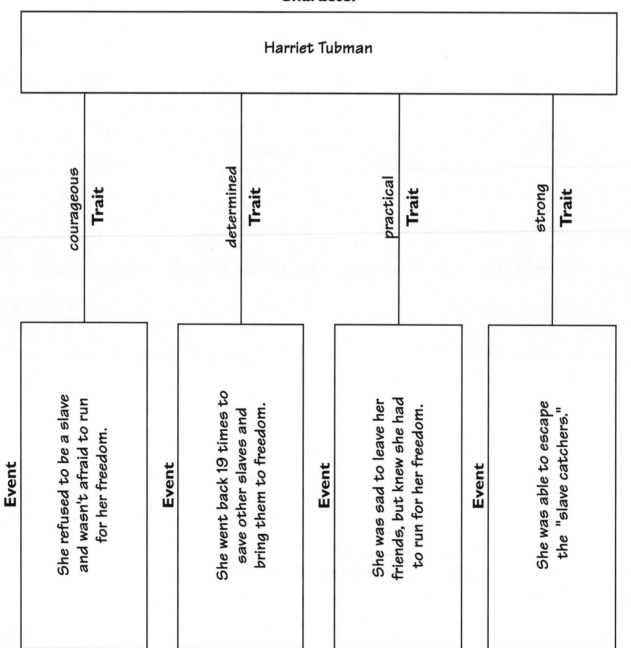

Harriet Tubman

Trait _courageous_

Trait _determined_

Trait _practical_

Trait _strong_

Event _She refused to be a slave and wasn't afraid to run for her freedom._

Event _She went back 19 times to save other slaves and bring them to freedom._

Event _She was sad to leave her friends, but knew she had to run for her freedom._

Event _She was able to escape the "slave catchers."_

Write your description on the lines below. If you need more space, continue writing on a separate sheet of paper.

Students should describe Tubman as courageous, determined, and practical. They

should support their answer with details from the poem.

Standards 1,2,3,4,5,6,7

_____

_____

_____

_____

_____

_____

_____

_____

_____

Hint Analyze a character by describing character traits. Look at the traits you wrote on the Character Traits Web. Use those traits and the examples you found to write your essay. After you finish, remember to use the checklist on page 56 to help you review your writing.

Speak Out

You have read about an American who is remembered for courageously helping others. Who is someone in U.S. history you admire for a similar reason? Prepare a short speech about this person. Then give your speech to the class.

DIRECTIONS: Read these two stories. The first is an adaptation of a well-known Greek myth. The second is a story about a girl who learns a hard lesson. Then answer questions 25 through 30. Darken the circle at the bottom of the page or write your answer on the lines.

Daedalus and Icarus

One day, for no reason, the king had Daedalus imprisoned. Daedalus was clever, so he escaped from his cell. He disguised himself, took shelter in an empty hut, and sent for his son Icarus. But he knew it would take a great deal of cleverness to escape from the island.

Each day Daedalus watched the seagulls flying overhead. He *envied* their freedom. After weeks of watching, he came up with a plan.

From dawn to midday Daedalus and Icarus looked for gull feathers. Icarus found the search amusing. Daedalus did not. During the afternoon Daedalus would work with thread, wax, and feathers. Finally, the pairs of wings were finished. Daedalus put them on his shoulders and tried them out. After several tries, he learned to fly. Now it was time to teach Icarus to fly.

"Icarus," Daedalus said sternly, "you must listen carefully to what I'm about to say. There is a great danger to flying. If you fly too low, the moisture close to the earth will increase the weight of the feathers and you will fall. If you fly too close to the sun, its heat will melt the wax that holds the feathers together—"

"And I'll fall?" Icarus interrupted.

"Yes, my son," the father replied.

The day of their escape arrived. They took off. The two were quickly driven apart by the sea breezes. Sadly, a boy with wings that allow him to fly with birds quickly forgets such things as warnings. Soon Icarus had risen into air warm enough to melt the wax. Daedalus, his cleverness of no use to him now, watched as his son fell to the sea.

Glittering Diamonds

Mr. Robbins was cooking hot dogs over a campfire when his daughter approached. "No, Kristin. I haven't changed my mind," he said. He knew what she was going to ask.

"But, Dad—" Kristin began.

"Look," Mr. Robbins said, "those kids who plan to hike on The Rock tonight are three and four years older than you. You're ten years old. I want you to turn eleven in one piece."

"But, Dad. You know how bright it is on The Rock when there's a full moon! That's why those kids are going tonight. It'll be almost like daylight, except that in the daytime you can't see the diamonds glittering. And it's only at night you can hear the ghosts groaning."

"That's quartz glittering. And those groaning sounds are simply the contracting of rock as it cools after having expanded all day in the heat."

"But—"

"Enough." Mr. Robbins cut his daughter off. He was running out of patience.

Kristin was quiet while she and her dad ate hot dogs. Mr. Robbins pointed out Kristin's favorite constellations. Kristin usually got excited about stargazing. But tonight her mind was somewhere else.

After she helped her dad clean up, she said, "Is it okay if I go hang out with that boy I met at the creek today? We said we'd try to meet at the playground after dinner."

"Fine with me," Mr. Robbins said. "But be back in about an hour. We can't stay up too late if we want to wake up with the sun for a full day of hiking tomorrow."

Kristin walked off slowly. But as soon as she got out of her dad's sight, she dashed to the meeting place of the group going on the full-moon hike. She knew it was later than the planned time—but not by much. "Maybe they won't leave on time," she thought.

She walked up just in time. "You almost got left behind," said a boy named Marshall. "Let's go."

The group started up the main trail to The Rock's summit. Halfway to the top, the leader left the trail and took off through the trees and brush. Everyone followed her.

Kristin paused to hear The Rock's groaning sounds but decided it must be too early. It wasn't too early to see the diamonds glittering in the moonlight. They were diamonds to her—no matter what her dad said. She felt a twinge of guilt in her chest for disobeying her father, but she shook off the feeling.

"Hey, guys, wait up!" she yelled and started running to catch up with the flashlight beam.

She didn't see the tree root and hadn't realized that she'd been walking close to the edge of a sharp drop-off. Suddenly, she felt herself falling...

"Mr. Robbins. Come quick! Kristin's over here." Kristin saw her dad crying and laughing at the same time.

"I'm sorry, Dad," Kristin whimpered.

"Shh. You're still in one piece. And that's all that matters right now." Mr. Robbins helped carry Kristin back to their car. On the way, Kristin wondered if she'd ever be back to hear The Rock groan again.

25 Which of the following tells you that the first story could not have really happened?

A A man and his son could not collect so many feathers.

B The heat of the sun could not melt wax.

C Even wearing large wings, people cannot fly as birds do.

D A man cannot escape a prison cell.

Hint Identify what is real and what is not real. A myth is a traditional story that usually describes deeds of gods and men. Impossible events occur often in them. Which choice sounds like an impossible event?

26 The boxes show some things that happened in the second story.

Kristin asks her dad if she can meet a boy at the playground.		Kristin rushes to catch up with the group.
1	2	3

Which event belongs in Box 2?

F Mr. Robbins points out constellations to Kristin.

G Kristin is seriously injured from a fall.

H Mr. Robbins tells Kristin she is too young to hike on The Rock at night.

J Kristin feels a twinge of guilt.

Hint Put the events in order. Find each event in the story. In what order did the events happen?

27 What does *envied* mean as it is used in the first story?

A copied   C enjoyed

B wished he had   D hoped to end

Hint This is a vocabulary question. Find where this sentence is located. A clue to the meaning of this word can be found in what happens later in the story.

Answers

25 Ⓐ Ⓑ ● Ⓓ	26 Ⓕ Ⓖ Ⓗ ●	27 Ⓐ ● Ⓒ Ⓓ
Standards 1,2,3,11	**Standards 1,3**	**Standards 1,2,3,6**

28 In the first story, the author said, "Icarus found the search amusing. Daedalus did not." Why doesn't Daedalus enjoy the search?

Answers should include that Icarus thought that the search was a game. But

Daedalus knew that their only hope of escape depended on the success of the

search.

Standards 1,2,3,4,5,6

Hint Determine meaning by using the information in the story. Look for the scene where Icarus and Daedalus are searching for feathers. Reread the part of the story that follows this.

29 What will Kristin probably do in the future when her father tells her that she cannot do something that she wants to do?

Possible answer: Since Kristin was injured when she went hiking at night after her

father told her not to, she will be more likely to listen to her father in the future.

Standards 1,3,4,5,6,11

 Hint This question asks you to predict what will happen. Use your own judgment and experiences, as well as what you have learned about Kristin from the story to make a prediction.

30 Compare and contrast the two stories. Discuss their themes, settings, main characters, and conclusions. Include many details from the stories.

 A Venn Diagram can help you organize the information you need to write this essay. Label each oval with a story title. List the differences in the outside parts. List how they are the same in the overlapping parts.

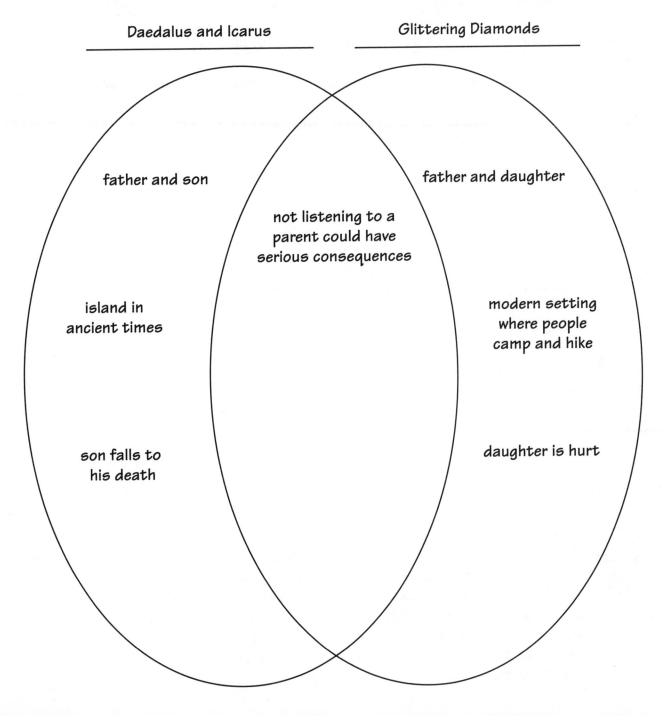

Daedalus and Icarus

Glittering Diamonds

father and son

not listening to a parent could have serious consequences

father and daughter

island in ancient times

modern setting where people camp and hike

son falls to his death

daughter is hurt

Write your essay on the lines below. If you need more space, continue writing on a separate sheet of paper.

Answers will vary. Students should include many details from the stories. Similarities

between the stories include the following:

Theme: not listening to a parent may have serious consequences

Differences between the stories include the following:

Main characters: a father and son versus a father and daughter

Setting: an island in ancient times versus a modern location for camping and hiking

Conclusion: the son falls to his death versus the daughter is hurt

Standards 1,2,3,4,5,6,7

Hint Compare and contrast the two stories by identifying details and making connections between the passages. Look at the information you filled in on the Venn Diagram. Use it to write your essay. Write one paragraph on the similarities between the two stories. Write another paragraph about the differences between them. After you finish, use the checklist on page 56 to make sure your writing is the best it can be.

UNIT 4

Introduction—Test

Unit 4 provides an actual reading test. This unit may be used as a test to assess students' learning and/or to simulate formal tests. The test includes six reading selections from various genres. The first four passages are each followed by multiple-choice and short-answer questions, as well as an essay question. The last two passages, which are linked, are followed by one set of questions. The test questions represent the three levels of comprehension (literal, interpretive, and critical).

Test-Taking Guidelines

Familiarize students with the following important test principles:

1. Time Use
► Not spending too much time on any one question
► Working rapidly but comfortably
► Marking items to return to if time permits
► Using any time remaining to review answers

2. Error Avoidance
► Paying careful attention to directions
► Determining clearly what is being asked
► Marking multiple-choice answers in the appropriate place on the answer sheet and writing answers to open-ended questions on the lines provided
► Checking all answers if time permits
► Being neat and avoiding making stray marks

3. Reasoning
► Reading the entire passage carefully to gain comprehension
► Reading the entire question and all the choices before answering a multiple-choice question
► Trying to eliminate known incorrect answer choices before answering a multiple-choice question
► Reading the entire question and noting what is needed for an open-ended question
► Applying what has been learned

Administering the Test

To simulate a formal reading test, take the following steps on the day of the test:

► Hang a "Do Not Disturb—Testing" sign on the classroom door to avoid interruptions.

► Seat students at an appropriate distance from one another, and make sure that their desks are clear of all materials.

► Provide students with sharpened pencils that have erasers.

► Keep supplies, such as extra pencils and paper readily available.

► Make sure that the students' books are opened to the directions on page 89, and go over the directions with them.

Before they begin, familiarize students with the Answer Sheet in the back of the Student Book. Remind students to press firmly with their pencils to make a dark mark on the Answer Sheet for the multiple-choice questions. Also remind them of the importance of completely filling in the answer spaces and erasing any stray marks. Tell them to write their answers to the short-answer and essay questions in the Student Book on the lines provided.

While you are administering the test, make sure that students understand the directions before proceeding. Circulate around the classroom, making sure that students are following the directions, that they are working on the appropriate test, and that they are marking and writing their answers properly.

The following pages are picked up from Unit 4 in the Student Book for Level E. The correct answers to the multiple-choice questions have been filled in on the Answer Sheet on page 127 of this guide. Possible answers to the short-answer questions and requirements for the essay answers are given directly after each individual question.

Test

You will now be taking a practice test. The test includes all the skills you have reviewed in this book. Follow the directions in each section. As always, remember to use the **Four *R*s: R**eady, **R**ead, **R**espond, **R**eview. You may look back at the reading passages as needed.

For the multiple-choice questions, work carefully and try to get as many questions right as you can. Do not spend too much time on any one question. If you are not sure of an answer, make the best choice you can and go on to the next question. You can go back and check answers later if you have time.

For the open-ended questions, plan out what you want to say before writing. Use graphic organizers to help you write your essay questions. Make sure that you respond to all parts of each question. After you finish writing, use the checklist on page 56 to help you review your work.

DIRECTIONS: Read this story about a boy who gets lost. Then answer questions 1 through 11. Darken the circle on the separate answer sheet or write your answer on the lines.

Lost but Not Forgotten

by Stephen Wallenfels

Dad said this could happen.

I never believed him. But he was right.

So here I am, smack-dab in the middle of it. All alone. No one to help me but myself.

Two questions come to mind as I sit under this tree, freezing in the snow.

How did I get here, and why me?

The first answer is pretty simple. I got lost.

Actually it's more complicated than that. I didn't pay attention to the boundary signs. I thought the snow looked pretty good. So I told my friend Benito that I'd meet him at the bottom of the hill in twenty minutes.

How was I to know a blizzard was coming?

How was I to know that my tracks would disappear?

As for the second question, the answer is obvious. Why me? Because I'm always doing stupid things. Opening my mouth when I should keep it shut. Breaking things I shouldn't be touching. And in this case, wandering off where I had no business going.

If Dad were here, I know exactly what he'd be saying.

I told you this would happen, Deke. Now what are you going to do about it?

The snow just won't stop falling. It's getting harder to see, and I'm tired of walking. I'm tired of yelling. With all this snow it's like yelling HELP! into a pillow. No one will hear me. So now I'm sitting under a tree, watching the snow pile up on my clothes. I can barely see my snowboard. It's a gray shadow in a curtain of white.

What would it be like, I wonder, freezing to death?

Don't just sit there. Build a cave.

That's what Dad would say. But he died in a hospital bed, so he can't say anything to me anymore.

Build a cave.

"With what?" I say. "I don't have a shovel. My hands are freezing."

There must be something you can use.

I look around. All I see are snow-covered trees.

Come on, Deke. Use your head.

"Like I'm going to dig a cave with my head? I don't think so."

Then it hits me. The snowboard.

I get up. My legs are stiff. My teeth are clacking together like marbles in a sack.

Look for the side of a hill.

"I know. I know."

I start to dig. The snowboard works OK. My gloves are wet. After a while my hands feel like wooden blocks. It's time to take a rest. I'm kind of sleepy.

Don't stop. Keep digging the cave. You need shelter from the wind.

My eyes open. There's hardly any light. A wind has come up. It's whipping the snow, stinging my face.

"OK, I'll keep digging. But only for a while."

Keep digging until you're done.

That's what Dad would have said. Clean your room. Mow the lawn. Finish your math. Don't stop until you're done.

Now it's too dark to see, but I think the cave is finished. I don't have enough room to sit up. I can't stretch out, and the floor's all lumpy. The wind howls outside. But inside the cave it's quiet. Like in a fort made of mattresses. I curl up into a ball and close my eyes. A stupid kid, thirsty and alone, shivering on a bed made of snow.

I try to think of someplace warm. I think of Cancun. It's a place Dad promised to take us. A beautiful beach in Mexico. He'd bring home pictures of white sand and blue-green water. Tanned people in bathing suits. But Dad got too sick and we never went. I still have the pictures in my bedroom. . . .

Wake up. You need air.

"But I want to sleep."

You forgot to make a vent.

"You make a vent. I'm too tired."

My eyes jolt open. There's been a sharp pain in my leg, as if I'd been kicked with a size-twelve boot. Suddenly I need to stretch out. I feel my boots punching through snow. A cold burst of air rushes in. It tastes good. I breathe deeply, then twist around and peek outside. The wind has stopped. The snow has stopped. Stars shine down through the trees.

I can sleep now. I close my eyes and hope that the sun will come up soon.

Time for school, Deke. Get up. You'll miss the bus.

"Let me sleep for five more minutes."

I hear the bus. It's coming.

There is a sound. A strange sound; a familiar sound. My eyes open again, and I'm surrounded by a blue-white light. And the sound—I recognize the *thwopp-thwopp-thwopp.* Something big in the air. Then, under the noise, someone is yelling. A voice echoes through the trees.

"Deke!"

Screaming, I explode out of the cave. The sun is shining. I see something moving. A person. Someone wearing an orange jacket and a backpack. On snowshoes.

"I'm here!" I yell. "Over here!"

The person waves and comes running toward me.

I look around. My snowboard is buried. The ground is white and perfectly smooth except for where I burst out of the snow.

And except for one spot near the door.

It looks like a footprint. A big footprint.

It reminds me of a size-twelve boot.

1 Which of these sentences from the story contains a simile?

    A I can't stretch out, and the floor's all lumpy.

    B After a while my hands feel like wooden blocks.

    C My eyes open again, and I'm surrounded by a blue-white light.

    D What would it be like, I wonder, freezing to death?

2 At the end of the story, Deke sees a spot in the snow that reminds him of a size-twelve boot. Whose boot is he thinking of?

    F His own

    G His friend Benito's

    H His father's

    J The rescue worker's

3 What is the setting of the story?

    A A boy who gets lost in a blizzard

    B A boy who survives by following the advice of his father

    C In modern times in an area with cold winters

    D In the last century in an area with cold winters

4 What is the *best* explanation for the story's title?

    F Deke gets lost, but his friend Benito does not forget to tell someone to rescue Deke.

    G Deke no longer has his father, but his father's presence in his memory helps him survive.

    H Deke thinks he has lost the ability to dig a cave, but in a crisis he realizes that he has not forgotten how.

    J Deke loses his way in the forest because he has forgotten to pay attention to the boundary signs.

5 Which of these is the *best* statement of the story's theme?

   A In risky situations you must always stay calm.

   B Never do anything halfway.

   C A good friend will help bring you home if you get lost.

   D The people we love live on through us even after they're gone.

6 One piece of advice that Deke imagines coming from his father is "Come on, Deke. Use your head." What does this mean?

   F Put some effort into thinking.

   G Use your head as a shovel.

   H Look through the trees.

   J Think about someplace warm.

7 The boxes show some things that happened in the story.

A wind starts blowing that stings Deke's face.		Deke punches through the snow with his boots.
1	2	3

Which event belongs in Box 2?

   A Deke hears a strange but familiar sound.

   B Deke sits under a tree and watches the snow pile up on his clothes.

   C Deke starts to dig a cave using his snowboard.

   D Deke thinks about a beach in Mexico.

8 There is enough information in the story to conclude that—

   F Deke's father had traveled to Mexico

   G Deke will not risk getting lost in a blizzard again

   H Deke's mother is yelling his name at the end

   J Benito is probably also lost in the snow

9 Why would someone in Deke's situation try to think about someplace warm?

A person suffering from intense cold might think of a warm place to take his or
her mind off the discomfort.

Standards 1,3,4,5,6,11

10 What lesson has Deke learned from this experience?

Deke has learned to be more aware of his surroundings, to not give up in bad
situations, and to remember his father's advice.

Standards 1,3,4,5,6

I I Write a summary of the story. Be sure to include only the most important events and details.

Use a graphic organizer to plan your summary.

Write your summary on the lines below. If you need more space, continue writing on a separate sheet of paper.

Possible answer: A boy does not pay attention to the boundary lines when he is going to meet his friend to go snowboarding. He gets lost in a blizzard. He survives by listening to the advice his father would have given him if he were still alive. He uses his snowboard to dig a cave, and he makes a vent so he can have air to breathe. He is rescued the next morning. As he leaves his cave, he sees a footprint that is the same size that his father's was.

Standards 1,3,4,5,6,7

DIRECTIONS: Read this poem about a girl who finds something special while visiting her grandmother. Then answer questions 12 through 22. Darken the circle on the separate answer sheet or write your answer on the lines.

Summers at Grandma's

by Sharon Chmielarz

Not much to do summers at Grandma's,
her little house on a dusty road,
a lane no cars come down
anymore. It's good for walking
and collecting. Stones, yes,
but glass, too, pieces so old
the edges are smooth as jewels—
Once I found an amber clear as nectar.

Shards Grandma calls them,
crockery and such the road grader
turns up, pieces of treasures broken
when they fell from **emigrants'** wagons.
I wonder what the amber held,
some Persian perfume? And whose
it was? I can almost see through the shard,
a girl like me before a mirror no longer here.

emigrants = people who leave one country to live in another

12 How does the speaker feel about the road by her grandmother's house?

   A She thinks it is dusty and boring.

   B She thinks it is old and special.

   C She enjoys watching the cars on the road.

   D She wishes someone would repair the road.

13 Which of the following is probably *most* important to the speaker?

   F Walking on the road every day to get fresh air and exercise

   G Finding out who the emigrant girl was who used to own the amber

   H Thinking about the meaning behind objects she finds

   J Sharing her adventures with her grandmother

14 The phrase "clear as nectar" is an example of—

   A a metaphor

   B a simile

   C personification

   D hyperbole

15 Which of the following can you *most* likely conclude from the poem?

   F The speaker wishes she lived in the past.

   G The speaker likes visiting her grandmother.

   H The speaker likes summers.

   J The speaker does not live in the country year-round.

16 What is the mood of the poem?

    A joyous

    B desperate

    C thoughtful

    D sad

17 Which of these was directly responsible for the girl finding the things she did on the road?

    F Emigrants traveled on her grandmother's road in wagons.

    G Her grandmother invited her to visit.

    H She went to collect stones.

    J Her grandmother's road was worked on with a road grader.

18 Another word for *shards* is—

    A mirrors

    B treasures

    C pieces

    D rocks

19 Which of these statements would the author *most* likely make?

    F Objects can be links to the past.

    G Crockery is valuable.

    H A road is a fun place to play.

    J Children were different in the past.

20 What is the setting of the poem?

The poem takes place on a road by a girl's grandmother's house in modern times.

Standards 1,2,3,4,5,6

_____

_____

_____

_____

_____

_____

21 The poem says "I can almost see through the shard, a girl like me before a mirror no longer here." What does this mean?

It means the girl can imagine that the shard was once part of a mirror owned by a

little girl who is like her.

Standards 1,2,3,4,5,6

_____

_____

_____

_____

_____

22 A character sketch is a description of someone's personality. It includes details and examples to explain what the person is like. Write a character sketch of the girl in the poem. You may have to draw conclusions about the girl's personality.

Use a graphic organizer to plan your character sketch.

Write your character sketch on the lines below. If you need more space, continue writing on a separate sheet of paper.

Answers will vary. Students may say that the girl likes to collect things and that she

is curious and thoughtful, as evidenced by her wondering about the long-ago owners of

the objects she has found. She is also imaginative because she is able to entertain

herself and easily imagine the owner of the amber to be a girl like herself.

Standards 1,2,3,4,5,6,7

_____

_____

_____

_____

_____

_____

_____

_____

_____

_____

_____

DIRECTIONS: Read this article about an amazing rescue mission. Then answer questions 23 through 33. Darken the circle on the separate answer sheet or write your answer on the lines.

The Great Penguin Rescue

by Renee Skelton

The news spread like wildfire. Thousands of penguins off the South African coast were in danger of dying. The culprit: an oil spill from a sinking ship. If the birds were going to survive, they needed help fast. Oil coated the beaches and soiled the waters around Robben and Dassen islands, where the African penguins live. Many birds were suffering, covered with a thick layer of oil goo. Others were already dead.

Luckily, volunteers rushed to the area from all over the world. Many went straight to the islands, where they worked feverishly to keep the birds from entering the oily sea. They scooped up adults first and then went back to rescue the chicks. For days volunteers loaded penguins into cardboard boxes for a short boat or helicopter ride to the mainland.

Everyone moved as fast as they could, because oil can kill penguins quickly. It removes the natural waterproofing of their feathers. When an oiled bird enters the water to fish, it gets soaked to the skin. Its body temperature can drop dangerously low. And when penguins swallow the toxic oil, it poisons and often kills them.

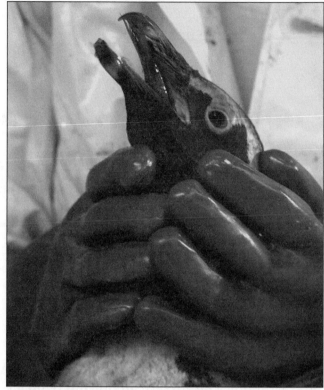

Trying their hardest to save the birds, thousands of volunteers worked tirelessly. A bird relocation this large had never before been attempted. It was a huge job. Workers moved 40,000 penguins off the islands. Then the action shifted to the mainland, where penguin sorting took place. Unoiled birds went to Port Elizabeth for immediate release. Oiled birds were sent to centers in and around Cape Town for care and cleaning.

For the first couple of days after the oiled birds' arrival, volunteers kept them fed and warm. Once the penguins were strong enough, they got a good scrubbing in basins of soapy water to clean off every bit of oil.

The birds remained captive for another two or three weeks while they preened: With their beaks, the birds spread natural oil from a gland under their tails onto their feathers. This is what makes penguins waterproof and was a crucial step before the birds could safely swim home—the ultimate goal of the rescue team. Volunteers tested the birds in pools of water, checking the feathers to make sure water would bead up on them and roll off. After passing this test and getting checked to make sure they were disease-free, the birds were returned to the now clean, oil-free islands.

The oil spill could have spelled disaster for this *vulnerable* penguin species. "Forty percent of the African penguin population was affected by the spill," says Steve Sarro, a penguin expert from the U.S. who answered the call for help. "If we had lost these birds, we could have lost this species in the wild."

Oil and birds don't mix, but in a crisis, people and penguins certainly do.

23 You can tell that *vulnerable* means—

A fortunate

B difficult

C easily affected

D hard to find

24 According to the article, what did the penguins have to do before they could swim safely home?

F Return to their normal body temperature

G Spread an oil that they produce onto their feathers

H Begin eating enough to survive

J Prove that their strength had returned

25 Read these sentences from the article.

Thousands of penguins off the South African coast were in danger of dying. The culprit: an oil spill from a sinking ship.

Which of the following appears in these sentences?

A hyperbole   C metaphor

B personification   D simile

26 The purpose of the penguin sorting that took place on the mainland was to separate—

F birds who had successfully preened themselves from birds who had not

G dying birds from healthy birds

H disease-free birds from birds with diseases

J birds with no oil on them from birds with oil on them

27 If you were writing a summary of the article, which of the following ideas would be *least* important to include?

   A Trying their hardest to save the birds, thousands of volunteers worked tirelessly.

   B They scooped up adults first and then went back to rescue the chicks.

   C Thousands of penguins off the South African coast were in danger of dying.

   D And when penguins swallow the toxic oil, it poisons and often kills them.

28 Before penguins could be moved from centers around Cape Town to the oil-free islands, all of these had to happen *except*—

   F sorting oiled and unoiled birds

   G allowing them time to preen

   H checking for diseases

   J making sure that their feathers were once again waterproofed

29 What was the author's purpose in writing this article?

   A To entertain readers with an exciting tale about penguins

   B To make an argument that oil and birds do not mix

   C To describe the events of an unusual rescue mission

   D To persuade readers to try to save penguins

30 Which of these generalizations can be made based on this article?

   F Any time wildlife is injured by oil spills people will join in a rescue.

   G The African penguin population will eventually become extinct.

   H Any time penguins come in contact with oil they will need help from people.

   J When oil is spilled from a ship, penguins will suffer.

31 Explain what the author means when she says, "Oil and birds don't mix, but in a crisis, people and penguins certainly do."

Oil and birds don't mix because oil either damages or kills penguins. Usually,

people and penguins don't mix because penguins are wild and fearful of humans;

but in a crisis, penguins may need the help of humans.

Standards 1,3,4,5,6,11

32 Describe the mood of the article. What are some words and phrases from the article that help to create this mood?

The author has created a mood that is very dramatic. It presents a sense of

urgency and of things happening fast—just as they did in reality. Various

examples of phrases from the article may be used.

Standards 1,3,4,5,6

33 Write a newspaper article for a school paper in which you summarize the events of the penguin rescue. Since your newspaper article must be much shorter than the article you just read, you must carefully choose the events and details you include.

Use a graphic organizer to plan your article.

Write your article on the lines below. If you need more space, continue writing on a separate sheet of paper.

Answers will vary. Students should include the most important points of the article

and not include unimportant details.

Standards 1,3,4,5,6,7,12

_____

_____

_____

_____

_____

_____

_____

_____

_____

_____

_____

_____

_____

DIRECTIONS: Read this story about a boy who has to make big changes in his life. Then answer questions 34 through 44. Darken the circle on the separate answer sheet or write your answer on the lines.

Guppies and Puppies

Paul didn't know what his dad was talking about when he came through the door on a warm March day and announced that he was being transferred to a new job.

"What do you mean, *transferred*?" Paul asked his dad.

"I mean we're moving to Michigan when school is out."

"Michigan!" Paul was shocked. He knew Michigan was at the top of the map. Florida, where he lived with his mom and dad and an aquarium full of guppies, was at the very bottom.

"Just think," Paul's dad said. "Not many months after we get settled into our new home, there will be snow on the ground. We can buy you a sled and build snowmen."

At the time, Paul couldn't think about snow. He didn't want to leave his school or his best friend Hector. And what about his aquarium? Baby guppies had just been born, and they were so small. They wouldn't live through a long drive to Michigan.

Paul got the guppies because he couldn't have a puppy. He had begged his parents for a dog, but they said no. As long as Paul's family lived in an upstairs apartment, it just wasn't possible. Paul's grandmother had given him an aquarium and a plastic bag of fish instead. Paul enjoyed watching the fish grow, but he'd still wanted a puppy.

Hector knocked on his door. Hector's sister Maria and their dog Ruffles were with him.

"You want to walk to the store for ice cream?" Hector asked.

"Sure." But Paul wasn't in the mood for ice cream. Ruffles ran circles around him and yelped. He shoved her away.

"Paul, you know she just had puppies. You shouldn't do that." Maria said. "What's the matter?"

"My dad's getting transferred to Michigan."

"Michigan! It snows there! I've never seen snow," Hector said.

After they bought ice cream, the spring heat started melting them. So the three of them sat in the shade. Paul felt like his heart was melting as fast as his ice cream. He ended up letting Ruffles lick his cone.

A few weeks later, Paul's mom told him that he needed to decide what to do with his fish before they left for Michigan.

"I'm sorry, honey," she said. "But I don't think they would survive the trip."

Paul rested his head against the cool glass of his aquarium. His mom asked "Would you like me to take care of it for you?"

"No," Paul said. He knew he had to find a good home for his guppies.

The next morning he approached his mother. "Mom, here's the plan. I'll give my aquarium and the guppies to Hector and Maria. I'm sure they'll want them. They'll take good care of them because they take such good care of Ruffles and her puppies. Hector can e-mail me if he has any trouble." Paul left the kitchen. He was pleased that he had come up with such a great idea.

It was hard work moving the aquarium. Paul's dad helped him bring everything over to Hector's house. Then Paul helped Hector set up the aquarium in his bedroom. As Paul was saying goodbye to Hector and Maria, Ruffles barked at him like she knew he wouldn't be coming back. He was going to miss Ruffles.

"I think Ruffles is trying to say you're forgetting something," Hector's mom said. When Paul looked up, they were all smiling at him.

"Here!" Maria called out from behind Paul. She had a squirming puppy in her arms. "Ruffles wants you to have this one."

Paul looked at his dad. He expected his father to tell him to give the puppy back. But his dad said, "Your mom and I decided that since we're going to have a back yard in Michigan, you should have a dog. Hector's family really wanted you to have one of Ruffles' puppies."

Hector smiled and said, "You can e-mail me about how the puppy is doing. I'll e-mail you about how to take care of him."

The following March, Paul and his friend Amelia were sledding on a hill with their dogs. Every time Paul and Amelia zoomed down the hill, the dogs would run after the sleds.

Later, after Amelia had gone home, Paul e-mailed Hector. He told him all about sledding and how he'd learned that no two snowflakes are alike—that each is special in its own way. As he typed the words, Paul smiled at his dog laying by his feet.

34 The sentence, "Paul felt like his heart was melting as fast as their ice cream," is an example of—

   A hyperbole

   B simile

   C metaphor

   D personification

35 Why did Paul decide to give his guppies to Hector and Maria?

   F Paul knew that they took good care of their dog Ruffles and her puppies.

   G They lived close by, so the guppies would not have to travel far.

   H Hector had told Paul that he wished he could have a fish tank with guppies.

   J Paul hoped that they would give him a puppy if he gave them the guppies.

36 What made Paul's parents change their minds about letting their son have a dog?

   A They saw how much Paul loved Ruffles and her puppies.

   B They had talked to Hector's parents about owning a dog.

   C They thought Paul was now old enough to take care of a dog.

   D They were going to have a back yard in Michigan.

37 What is Paul's *main* problem in the story?

   F He knows he won't have a friend like Hector in Michigan.

   G He does not want to move to a place where it snows.

   H He has to leave everything that is familiar to him.

   J He is not allowed to get a puppy.

38 All of these words describe Paul in the first part of the story *except*—

    A disappointed

    B excited

    C frustrated

    D sad

39 Which of the quotes from the story is an *opinion*?

    F "They'll take good care of them [the guppies]."

    G "My dad's getting transferred to Michigan."

    H "I mean we're moving to Michigan when school is out."

    J "Hector's family really wanted you to have one of Ruffles' puppies."

40 What does Paul do after he sets up the aquarium in Hector's bedroom?

    A He walks to the store for an ice cream cone.

    B He tells his mother he has made an important decision.

    C He tells his father that he does not want to go to Michigan.

    D He takes one of Ruffles' puppies with him to Michigan.

41 Which of these sentences would fit *best* at the end of this story?

    F He told Hector that he really missed his guppies.

    G Hector might not care about snowflakes, but he cared about dogs.

    H Right now, he wanted to go play in the snow with his dog.

    J And he realized that the same was true about friends.

42 How does the puppy help Paul deal with moving?

A puppy is something that Paul has always wanted. It is also a connection to his

friends Hector and Maria.

Standards 1,3,4,5,6

_____

_____

_____

_____

43 What is the theme of this story?

Possible answer: Although we must make changes in our lives, we will always keep

our friends.

Standards 1,3,4,5,6

_____

_____

_____

_____

44 Compare and contrast Paul's life in Florida to his life in Michigan. Include many details from the story.

Use a graphic organizer to plan your essay.

Write your essay on the lines below. If you need more space, continue writing on a separate sheet of paper.

Based on details in the story, there are few similarities between Paul's life in Florida and his life in Michigan; in both places he has a friend and is happy. There are many differences between his life in Florida and his life in Michigan. He lived in an apartment in Florida and in a house with a back yard in Michigan. His friend is a boy in Florida and a girl in Michigan. He has guppies in Florida and a dog in Michigan. In March he was walking to the store in the heat to get ice cream; in Michigan in the same month of the year he is playing in the snow.

Standards 1,3,4,5,6,7

DIRECTIONS: First, read the article about exercise. Next read a handout given to students during the first meeting of an after-school class. Then answer questions 45 through 55. Darken the circle on the separate answer sheet or write your answer on the lines.

The Hows and Whys of Exercise

Did you know that it was probably a lot easier for your great-grandparents to get enough exercise than it is for you? When your great-grandparents were kids, they often walked wherever they needed to go. Their destinations were usually less than a mile or two away, within their small town or neighborhood. And transportation—cars, buses, and subways—was not readily available. Your great-grandparents also got more exercise because physical activity was often a part of their work and play. Many of our labor-saving machines weren't invented yet. So humans, including kids, did many of the necessary chores using muscle power. When kids had time to play, their games and sports were simple: tag, hide-and-seek, baseball, and basketball. They swam in a lake or river that they walked to.

How different life is today! Many of the places we want to go to are far from our homes. Since cars are so common, walking is thought of mainly as a form of enjoyment or exercise. Most of our chores are accomplished with little effort. Machines such as electric lawn mowers and vacuum cleaners do most of the work for us. In our spare time, we enjoy activities that require us to sit for long periods of time.

Nowadays it takes a big effort to get the physical activity your body needs. Is it worth the effort? Before you decide, take a look at these facts about exercise:

► Exercise helps you build up physical and mental power.

► Exercise helps you get rid of tension and stress.

► Aerobic exercises (vigorous activities like jogging and fast swimming) help your lungs and muscles—including your heart—work well and grow strong.

► Stretching-type exercises help you stay flexible and *agile*.

► Exercise reduces your chances of becoming overweight.

► Exercise reduces your risk of getting heart disease later in life.

You may already play a sport. You may already go skateboarding or shoot baskets in the park or go to a karate class. But if you don't, here are some suggestions for getting the exercise you need.

► Choose a physical activity that you like to do and that doesn't require a lot of skill. Do the activity gently and slowly at first. Then, over a period of time, do it more vigorously.

► Do a variety of physical activities so you're less likely to get bored. Do some physical activities that develop strength and others that develop flexibility.

► Begin a vigorous activity with a five-minute warm-up. The warm-up prepares the muscles, heart, and lungs for action. It also reduces the risk of injuries such as pulled muscles. End the activity with a five-minute cool-down. The cool-down gives your body time to get used to a lower level of activity.

► Remember that physical activity includes "everyday" activities as well as sports. Riding a bike, walking the dog, sweeping the house, raking the lawn, and climbing the stairs all get your body moving.

Exercise will make you feel good. It will give you energy for the things you like to do. It will help you stay healthy for years to come. And, finally, moving your body is simply fun.

S M A R T   M O V E S
AFTER-SCHOOL CLASS

Handout for Day 1: WHAT I DO IN MY FREE TIME

Directions for Days 1–7: At the end of each day (today is Day 1), record the number of hours you spend on each of the following activities. If you need to, use fractions of hours.

INACTIVE ACTIVITIES	DAY 1	DAY 2	DAY 3	DAY 4	DAY 5	DAY 6	DAY 7	TOTAL HOURS/WEEK
Watching TV								
Working at a computer								
Listening to music								
Talking to friends								
Reading								
Other _____								
Total Hours for the Day								
ACTIVE ACTIVITIES	DAY 1	DAY 2	DAY 3	DAY 4	DAY 5	DAY 6	DAY 7	TOTAL HOURS/WEEK
Walking								
Riding a bike								
Jogging or running								
Playing a sport								
Playing games								
Other _____								
Total Hours for the Day								

Directions for Day 8: Look at your totals for ACTIVE and INACTIVE activities for each day and for the week. Set a goal to increase the number of hours you do ACTIVE activities during the next 7 days.

My goal is to do_____ hours of ACTIVE activities during the next 7 days.

45 What would be another good title for "The Hows and Whys of Exercise"?

   A "Exercise and Your Muscles"

   B "How to Avoid Heart Disease"

   C "A Little Physical Activity for Your Heart"

   D "What Was Good for Your Great-Grandparents Is Good for You"

46 The author's purpose for writing the article is to—

   F describe ways to exercise that are fun

   G encourage readers to exercise, even though it may require effort

   H compare the level of exercise for past and present generations

   J list the reasons that exercise helps people stay healthy

47 You can tell that *agile* means—

   A healthy

   B strong

   C at the right weight

   D able to bend easily

48 Except in physical education class, Tomás does not exercise. But he has decided to start. According to the article, which of these should he do on the first day?

   F Run fast for half an hour

   G Jump rope at an easy pace

   H Play tennis until he works up a sweat

   J Join a soccer team

49 Which of these would you write in the "Other" blank under "Inactive Activities" on the after-school handout?

   A Dancing

   B Playing catch with a friend

   C Playing video games

   D Ice skating

50 With which statement would the author *least* likely agree?

   F Exercise is good for your body and mind.

   G Doing physical activity is worth the effort it often takes.

   H If you do the same type of exercise all the time, you may get tired of it.

   J In general, sports are a better form of exercise than everyday physical activities are.

51 According to the article, which of these is *not* a reason to warm up before doing vigorous exercise?

   A To get the lungs ready to work harder

   B To increase your flexibility

   C To cut down on the chances of getting injured

   D To prepare your muscles to work

52 Which of the following is an *opinion*?

   F Moving your body is simply fun.

   G Exercise helps your body develop correctly.

   H Some of our labor-saving machines weren't invented yet.

   J Getting enough exercise can make you feel good.

53 According to the article, why did our great-grandparents get more exercise than we do?

Our great-grandparents walked a lot more than we do since they often went

places that were closer to their homes and since transportation was not as

available. They also got exercise as they worked and played.

Standards 1,3,4,5,6

54 The author says, "In our spare time, we enjoy activities that require us to sit for long periods of time." Explain what the author means and give some examples of these activities.

Activities that kids often do in their spare time nowadays include watching TV,

watching movies at home or at a theater, playing video games, and working on a

computer. You are sitting down when you do all of these activities.

Standards 1,3,4,5,6,11

55 Imagine that you are a student at Beacon Hill Elementary School. You have read the article about exercise. And you recently completed the after-school class called "Smart Moves," which you believe has helped you a lot. Write a letter to your school principal telling why every fifth grader should take the class. Use information from the article and the handout.

Use a graphic organizer to plan your letter.

Write your letter on the lines below. If you need more space, continue writing on a separate sheet of paper.

Answers will vary. Students might mention how many kids do not get enough exercise

nowadays. They might indicate that the class was fun and interesting and that they

learned a lot of useful information. They should include some of the most important

points made in the article.

Standards 1,3,4,5,6,7,11,12

_____

_____

_____

_____

_____

_____

_____

_____

_____

_____

_____

Answer Sheet

STUDENT'S NAME			SCHOOL:

CUT HERE

LAST   **FIRST**   **MI**

TEACHER:

FEMALE ○   MALE ○

BIRTH DATE

MONTH	DAY	YEAR
Jan ○	⓪ ⓪	⑦ ⓪
Feb ○	① ①	⑧ ①
Mar ○	② ②	⑨ ②
Apr ○	③ ③	⓪ ③
May ○	④	④
Jun ○	⑤	⑤
Jul ○	⑥	⑥
Aug ○	⑦	⑦
Sep ○	⑧	⑧
Oct ○	⑨	⑨
Nov ○		
Dec ○		

GRADE ③ ④ ⑤ ⑥ ⑦ ⑧

Reading & Writing Excellence Level E

(Name grid columns A–Z with blank ovals at top)

TEST

1 Ⓐ ● Ⓒ Ⓓ	11 essay	21 short-answer
2 Ⓕ Ⓖ ● Ⓙ	12 Ⓐ ● Ⓒ Ⓓ	22 essay
3 Ⓐ Ⓑ ● Ⓓ	13 Ⓕ Ⓖ ● Ⓙ	23 Ⓐ Ⓑ ● Ⓓ
4 Ⓕ ● Ⓗ Ⓙ	14 Ⓐ ● Ⓒ Ⓓ	24 Ⓕ ● Ⓗ Ⓙ
5 Ⓐ Ⓑ Ⓒ ●	15 Ⓕ Ⓖ Ⓗ ●	25 Ⓐ ● Ⓒ Ⓓ
6 ● Ⓖ Ⓗ Ⓙ	16 Ⓐ Ⓑ ● Ⓓ	26 Ⓕ Ⓖ Ⓗ ●
7 Ⓐ Ⓑ Ⓒ ●	17 Ⓕ Ⓖ Ⓗ ●	27 Ⓐ ● Ⓒ Ⓓ
8 Ⓕ ● Ⓗ Ⓙ	18 Ⓐ Ⓑ ● Ⓓ	28 ● Ⓖ Ⓗ Ⓙ
9 short-answer	19 ● Ⓖ Ⓗ Ⓙ	29 Ⓐ Ⓑ ● Ⓓ
10 short-answer	20 short-answer	30 Ⓕ Ⓖ ● Ⓙ

31 short-answer	41 Ⓕ Ⓖ Ⓗ ●
32 short-answer	42 short-answer
33 essay	43 short-answer
34 Ⓐ ● Ⓒ Ⓓ	44 essay
35 ● Ⓖ Ⓗ Ⓙ	45 Ⓐ Ⓑ Ⓒ ●
36 Ⓐ Ⓑ Ⓒ ●	46 Ⓕ ● Ⓗ Ⓙ
37 Ⓕ Ⓖ ● Ⓙ	47 Ⓐ Ⓑ Ⓒ ●
38 Ⓐ ● Ⓒ Ⓓ	48 Ⓕ ● Ⓗ Ⓙ
39 ● Ⓖ Ⓗ Ⓙ	49 Ⓐ Ⓑ ● Ⓓ
40 Ⓐ Ⓑ Ⓒ ●	50 Ⓕ Ⓖ Ⓗ ●

51 Ⓐ ● Ⓒ Ⓓ
52 ● Ⓖ Ⓗ Ⓙ
53 short-answer
54 short-answer
55 essay

NCTE Standards for Test

Question	1	2	3	4	5	6	7	8	9	10	11	12
1	X		X			X						
2	X		X									
3	X		X									
4	X		X									
5	X		X									
6	X		X			X						
7	X		X									
8	X		X									
9	X		X	X	X	X					X	
10	X		X	X	X	X						
11	X		X	X	X	X	X					
12	X	X	X									
13	X	X	X								X	
14	X	X	X			X						
15	X	X	X									
16	X	X	X									
17	X	X	X									
18	X	X	X			X						
19	X	X	X								X	
20	X	X	X	X	X	X						
21	X	X	X	X	X	X						
22	X	X	X	X	X	X	X					
23	X		X			X						
24	X		X									
25	X		X			X						
26	X		X									
27	X		X								X	
28	X		X									
29	X		X								X	
30	X		X									
31	X		X	X	X	X					X	
32	X		X	X	X	X						
33	X		X	X	X	X	X					X
34	X		X			X						
35	X		X									
36	X		X									
37	X		X									
38	X		X									
39	X		X								X	
40	X		X									
41	X		X								X	
42	X		X	X	X	X						
43	X		X	X	X	X						
44	X		X	X	X	X	X					
45	X		X									
46	X		X								X	
47	X		X			X						
48	X		X									
49	X		X									
50	X		X								X	
51	X		X									
52	X		X								X	
53	X		X	X	X	X						
54	X		X	X	X	X					X	
55	X		X	X	X	X	X				X	X